D0722627

# Harper Joy

## Spokane's Man of Many Faces

# HARPER JOY

## Spokane's
## Man of Many Faces

 ## Let the Show Begin

by
Doris J. Woodward

Tony and Suzanne Bamonte
for the Spokane Corral of the Westerners
P.O. Box 8625
Spokane, WA 99203
(509) 838-7114

Copyright © 2007 by Doris J. Woodward
and/or
the Spokane Corral of the Westerners
and/or
Tornado Creek Publications
All rights reserved, including the rights to translate or reproduce this work or parts
thereof in any form or by media, without the written permission of the
author or publishers.

First published, 2007
Printed in the United States of America
by Walsworth Publishing and Printing Company
Marceline, Missouri, 64658

Library of Congress control number: 2007938617
ISBN-13 (hardbound): 9780974088174
*Pacific Northwesterner* ISSN 0030–882X

Cover picture from the Circus Room of the
Davenport Hotel

All photos from the Joy Collection
unless otherwise noted

Tornado Creek Publications
P.O. Box 8625
Spokane, WA 99203

# About the Author

**The author and Ed Joy at the family summer cottage on Liberty Lake, searching for potential book photos.** *(Bamonte photo)*

## Doris J. Woodward

Doris Woodward, born and raised in LaGrange, Illinois, was always interested in journalism, both in high school and at Michigan State University, but writing took a back seat for many years, thanks to marriage and raising four children.

Since that time, she has published numerous articles concerning a variety of interesting ancestors. Her first major subjects were Nathaniel Woodward, an early settler of Boston, Massachusetts; John McLucas, a Revolutionary War soldier; and two 19th century immigrants: Frederick Ecker and Matthew Fletcher. The Fletcher story received the 1998 National Genealogical Society first prize for family history writing.

She has also enjoyed researching and writing biographies of people who weren't related to her. In 2007, the *Pacific Northwesterner* published her article about General Thomas Tannatt and his wife Elizabeth, a story which received a third place award in 2006 from Westerners, International. In 2007, she received the National Historic Preservation Award from the National Society Daughters of the American Revolution. Meanwhile, a study and subsequent biography of Harper Joy proved to be irresistible to her. She felt it was a story that really needed to be told. She is now looking forward to finding another interesting man to write about but feels Harper Joy may be a hard act to follow!

# In Appreciation

In writing the story of Harper Joy, it is important to me to express my thanks to the following people for the help I have received:

• To Whitman College and their archives, where a fine collection of Harper Joy material can be found and which they gladly shared with me.

• To Robert "Pete" Reid, the Special Assistant to the President of Whitman, who was a good friend of Harper's and is still in touch with his children. Pete shared his memories of Harper and their connection with Phi Delta Theta, a fraternity that has been significant in my life as well.

• To the Northwest Museum of Arts and Culture in Spokane, and their archivists, Rose Krause and Jane Davey, who assisted me in the research and made it possible for the silent film *Crown Jewels* to be shown once again in the auditorium of the museum. Attendees included Nancy Joy and her son, Keys, from Maryland; Ed Joy and his wife Linda from Coeur d'Alene; Ben's daughter Cathleen from Alaska; Glenn Leitz from Fairfield; Shirley and Carl Drake from Diamond Lake; and from Spokane: Suzanne and Tony Bamonte, Marshall Shore, John and Joanne Happy, Henry Pierce and myself. It was a grand experience.

• To Tom McArthur, for providing us with so much valuable information about the Circus Room and for enabling us to visit it several times; also for sharing his enthusiasm for the Davenport Hotel and for proofreading the final manuscript.

• To Don Neraas, Spokane architect, for recalling his memories of Harper, and to Jim Wamble of Walla Walla, for furnishing stories and pictures of his mother, Gladys, who was Harper's half-sister.

• And, of course, to the Joy children: Ben, who, before his death, favored me with several wonderful long-distance calls from Alaska; Jim, whom I met early on in the research process at Liberty Lake and spoke to many times by phone; Nancy, who shared her memories with me both in the summer of 2006 and again in 2007; and Ed, who has continually supported the project, sharing all the terrific family pictures and wonderful memorabilia for me to use.

• And finally to Laura Arksey for proofreading and, of special importance, to Suzanne and Tony Bamonte for editing and being my cheerleaders through the entire project.

**Thanks from Doris Woodward**

*Signature drawing courtesy Don Neraas*

# Table of Contents

# HARPER JOY
## Why is his story important?

• Because he came from nothing and became somebody.

• Because he was successful in almost everything he did.

• Because he was a man whom people loved and respected.

• Because he was generous – with his time, talent and money.

• Because he left a significant legacy for the future.

• Because he approached life with a delightful sense of humor and loved to make people laugh.

AND IS THERE ANYTHING, REALLY, THAT IS BETTER THAN LAUGHTER?

*"Where are the clowns ...*
*There ought to be clowns ...*
*Send in the clowns!*
Stephen Sondheim

## Thank you, Harper!

# SNEAK PREVIEW

I have been interested in the name "Harper Joy" for many years, and I think it was preordained that I eventually write his story. Having lived in Spokane since 1962, it wasn't until 1978 that I moved to my present address on South Lincoln. The beautiful house and yard at 825 West Twenty-first Avenue just north of my property is the original Joy home. As a new neighbor, I had the pleasure of getting to know Dorothy Joy during the last years of her life. Although she didn't reminisce often about her husband, she did provide some charming glimpses of her family and earlier life. Dorothy was a woman of many interests. She loved the outdoors and reveled in the wildlife that existed in the woodsy lot that separated our two houses. Those woods are gone now, as is Dorothy, but my interest in the family has continued, and I felt their story needed to be told.

Those living in Spokane from the 1920s through the 1960s could hardly have avoided hearing about Harper Joy at some time. He was a dynamo of a man, who continually surprised his friends and family with his varied activities and whimsical sense of humor. He was interesting and complex, personally involved in a wide assortment of philanthropic and community organizations. His friends included many of Spokane's foremost citizens, as well as people in the investment and entertainment industries throughout the United States.

His story is one of diversity and fulfillment, but his first years were difficult and could have resulted in an entirely different life. However, good fortune smiled on him, as it often did throughout his life. He always seemed to be in the right place at the right time, among the right people, with the most fortunate results.

I have also included a section about the family of Harper's wife, Dorothy Mendenhall. Dorothy's grandfather, Henry Brook, contributed greatly to Spokane's early history. It is significant for me, in writing this article, to recognize his importance to this area. I believe the story of the Brook, Mendenhall and Joy families will be of value to future students of Inland Northwest history.

Researching these people has been a most delightful experience. I have had invaluable assistance from Harper's children and friends, without whom his story could never have been told. Fortunately, the family is heir to a vast collection of memorabilia, pictures, letters and newspaper articles that have enriched our knowledge of Harper Joy. One is astonished by the amount of material that is available about the life of this most versatile man.

Harper never did anything without giving it 100 percent, and many organizations were blessed with his enthusiastic participation. The reader can look forward to learning more about this remarkable man, whose accomplishments are legendary and whose sense of humor is a river that runs through all of them.

Welcome to the story of Harper Joy.

Doris J. Woodward
Spokane, Washington 2007

**Harper Joy**
**1894 – 1972**

*Isn't it strange that princes and kings,*
*And clowns that caper in sawdust rings,*
*And common folks like you and me,*
*Are builders for eternity?*
*To each is given a bag of tools,*
*A shapeless mass and a Book of Rules,*
*And each must fashion ere life has flown,*
*A stumbling block or a stepping stone*

The above poem was sent to Harper by Judge Carl C. Quackenbush

# The Curtain Rises
## Act One: THE SHOW BEGINS

As America was emerging from the 1890s to face the new and challenging 20th century, many young boys dreamed of some day running away from home to join the circus. It was an American dream – romantic and exciting. It was an escape from the ordinary. Of course, it was childish; it wasn't practical. So they eventually put their dreams away and moved on with their lives, becoming responsible adults. One of these boys, however, never quite forgot his dream, although he, too, put it behind him for many years. He became an exceptional businessman, a loving husband and father, and a respected pillar of his community. But eventually his dream returned, and the circus once again became an important part of his life. He was a unique person, a man of many talents, one of which was being a circus clown. Anyone who had the privilege of knowing him felt their lives had been enriched by the friendship. His name was Harper Joy, and Spokane, Washington, benefited immensely because he lived here.

### The Lounsbury Family

In order to understand Harper Joy, it is essential to examine his early years and the event that was to shape his later life. Harper Joy was not his birth name. He was born James Harper Lounsbury in Sedalia, Missouri, on August 31, 1894, the son of John Cape Lounsbury and Anna Harper. John and Anna came from interesting families, but it wasn't until Harper was an adult that he learned all the following details about his birth parents.

John Cape
Lounsbury,
Harper's birth
father, 1891.

His father was born February 19, 1868, in Illinois, the fifth child of James Calvin Lounsbury and Hannah Ann Merrill. James and Hannah were married in Cincinnati, Ohio, in 1849. James was a steamboat captain on the Ohio and Mississippi rivers and had a commission in the Union Navy during the Civil War. Hannah was a teacher in a women's seminary in Cincinnati at the time of their marriage.

James Harper Lounsbury's mother, Anna Harper, was born in June 1874 and later adopted by Josiah and Serena Harper. Her husband believed she was born of Irish parents, but this has not been verified. Josiah was a soldier in the Confederate Army, and after the war the family lived in Montserrat, Missouri, where he was a farmer and also a postmaster. Josiah Harper died in 1908 and is buried at Montserrat.

**Anna May Harper Lounsbury, 1891 Harper's birth mother.**

John Lounsbury and Anna Harper, who was only 17 years old at the time, were married in Montserrat on January 21, 1891, and moved to Sedalia, Missouri, soon after. John was a dispatcher for the Missouri Pacific railroad in that town. Three children were born to the Lounsburys in Missouri:

1. Eddie, born about 1892
2. a girl, stillborn
3. James Harper, born August 31, 1894

In February of 1895, John Lounsbury went west, settling in Walla Walla. Anna followed in April with the two boys. Their reason for moving is unknown but probably had something to do with John's job with the railroad. The trip must have been difficult for Anna, with two little boys, one of whom was less than eight months old. Add to this the fact that she was pregnant for the fourth time.

The family was finally reunited in Walla Walla, but disaster soon struck. Eddie, the older boy, was playing with matches, and his clothes caught on fire. His mother saw him at the top of the stairs but was unable to reach him in time. John Lounsbury was out of town at Winona, Washington, and heard of the tragedy at the same time he learned of the death of his father in Illinois, who died July 21, 1895, at the same hour of the same day as young Eddie.

Two months later, in September 1895, Anna gave birth to a daughter, whom they named Laura Irene. Soon after, John left his family for a job in Redding, California, never to return. He later claimed that he sent Anna the first $100 he was able to save, but the letter was returned to him unopened.

It may be easy today to criticize the way this couple dealt with a terrible situation. However, the tragedy had affected both parents deeply, and the circumstances understandably proved to be too much for them to handle. Anna was unable to care for her two remaining children, and the state stepped in to provide them with foster parents.

# A New Life in Walla Walla

Fortunately, James Harper and Laura Irene were too young to realize the full extent of the tragedy that had occurred. They were placed with a Walla Walla couple, Henry and Annie Joy, and although the children didn't know it at the time, it was a major turning point in their lives, for their foster parents were caring and responsible people who would have a tremendous impact on the lives of these hapless children.

Henry worked for the Oregon Washington Railway & Navigation Company (OWR&N), and Annie ran a boarding house for railroad workers. They had taken care of other foster children during their early years in Walla Walla and, in fact, had adopted one by the time the Lounsbury children came to them. They were not people of means, but they were people who cared.

Henry Macy Joy was born in 1854 on Nantucket Island, Massachusetts, the son of Reuben Glover Joy and Lydia Macy Joy. Lydia was the widow of Reuben's brother Alexander. Many of Henry's ancestors, like other Nantucket Islanders, were whaling men and traced their family back to Peter Joy and his wife, Sarah Goodwin, of Salem, Massachusetts. His mother's family, the Macys, were descendants of one of the earliest settlers of Nantucket and were possibly Quakers, as the break with the Puritan church of Massachusetts Bay was a prime reason for the settlement of this historic island.

**Henry and Annie Joy's home on Ninth Street in Walla Walla. It is no longer there.**

In the 1860 Nantucket census, Reuben is called a "mariner." He and Lydia are listed with Joseph, 17; William, 15; Eliza, 11; Edward, 9; Henry M., 6; and Obed, 3. By the 1870 census, the family was living in Rye, New York. Sons Joseph and William were no longer living with them and may have remained in Nantucket. Eliza was a school teacher; Edward and Henry M. were laborers. Obed 14, and Sarah are the youngest. By 1880 Reuben and Lydia had moved to Sutters Creek, California, where they were living by themselves.

Henry Joy's wife, Annie Laurie Littlefield, born on January 31, 1860, was also a descendant of an early New England family – the Littlefields of Maine. In 1859 the family sailed to California. There were two possible routes: one around the southern tip of South America and the other sailing to the Isthmus of Panama and portaging across to to the Pacific Ocean on the other side to board another ship bound for the California coast. (The Panama Canal was not completed until 1915.) Either way, it was a trip fraught with danger. Mrs. Littlefield was swept overboard in a storm, but fortunately the crew managed to save her, and she finally arrived in California to give birth to her daughter, Annie Laurie, a girl who was later to become the adoptive mother of Harper Joy.

Henry and Annie were married in Sutter's Creek in 1877 and four years later left California, going north via water to Wallula, Washington, and by train to Walla Walla. Sadly, the couple was not blessed with children, and Annie was lonesome for the family they had left behind. Taking in foster children proved to be a satisfying and worthy thing to do, and in those first years in Walla Walla the Joys provided care for some needy youngsters. Annie was deeply religious, a staunch member of the Methodist Church, and in later years active in the Woman's Christian Temperance Union and its work. In fact, in Harper Joy's family it was generally agreed that Annie considered herself to be the moral backbone of Walla Walla, Washington.

**Henry Macy Joy and Annie Littlefield Joy, Sutter's Creek, California, 1877.**

On December 8, 1883, a foster child, Harry Hess, was placed in the care of Henry and Annie. Harry had been born in Walla Walla on November 14, 1882, the son of Albert and Jennie Hess. Unfortunately, within a year his mother died, and his father was unable to take care of the baby. In June of 1884, the Joys legally adopted Harry, with his father's approval. His name was changed to Harry Hess Joy.

Henry and Annie must have made it known they wanted to care for other children besides Harry, as they were singled out by the authorities to take the Lounsbury children into their home about 1895 or 1896.

## The Adoptions

In later years, Harper Joy recalled the circumstances of his adoption. He remembered hiding behind the door in the Joy house and listening to Henry and Annie discussing the possibility of legally adopting him and his sister. Harper could only have been about three years old at the time, but it apparently made a tremendous impression upon him, for it was a story he passed on to his children.

Harper in 1897, age three, at the time of his adoption.

The Joys petitioned the court on November 12, 1897 to legally adopt the two Lounsbury children. In a lengthy document specifying the names, ages and natural parents of the two children, the statement is made that the said minors "have been living with and cared for by your petitioners, who by reason thereof have become attached to said children."

In a strange twist in the adoption proceedings, on November 21st, nine days after the Joys filed their petition, another petition was filed by Mary and William Fielden to adopt only Laura Irene, to which Anna Lounsbury, the biological mother, had consented. The case went back to court, and the original petition by the Joys was approved. Anna Lounsbury apparently appeared at this hearing and gave her consent. The Fielden adoption was set aside and nullified. The final adoption was filed in the Superior Court of Walla Walla County on December 30, 1897. At that time the children legally became James Harper Joy and Laura Irene Joy.

It was a happy and grateful family of five that converged that evening in the Joy home, for Henry and Annie now had three children, and the former Lounsbury children would not have to be separated. Harper never used the name "James." Annie preferred the name "Harper," as she felt "James" was too plebian. For many years he referred to himself as "J. Harper Joy," but his friends always called him "Harp." Likewise, Laura Irene dropped the "Laura" and was called simply "Irene."

# Anna Lounsbury and Another Baby Girl

Many questions about Harper's birth mother remain unanswered even today, but apparently she kept in contact with the Joys, at least for a while. On October 10, 1897, shortly before the above adoption proceedings, Anna gave birth to another baby girl, the father's name undisclosed.

Because Annie Joy had been involved in foster parenting, she was able to find a home for this new baby, who was placed with Eliza Jane and Acil Brotherton of Helix, Oregon, across the border from Walla Walla. The Brothertons named the baby Gladys Irene Bernice. Apparently they did not go through any formal adoption proceedings in the usual legal sense, but rather the baby was "taken in," a term that was sometimes used to indicate an informal adoption.

The Brotherons later divorced, and by 1910 Eliza Jane had married John Keyser. In the 1910 census of Lost Springs, Columbia County, Washington, the household includes John and Eliza Keyser with his stepdaughter, Gladys Brotherton, age 12. According to the 1920 census, the family was living in Starbuck, just 30 to 40 miles from Walla Walla, not far from her half-brother and sister.

Harper, Irene and Gladys all remembered playing together as children but were unaware of the relationship that existed. Gladys did not find out the circumstances of her birth until she was 12 years old, and even then Eliza Jane refused to talk about the details. Obviously Annie Joy and Eliza Jane Keyser wanted the

**Gladys Brotherton, 8th grade, Starbuck School. Gladys is 2nd from the left in the front row**. *(The following four photographs courtesy Jim Wamble)*

three children to be friends, because Gladys frequently came to Walla Walla from her home in Starbuck to play with the Joy children. Whether Anna Lounsbury had anything to do with this is not known, nor is it known when she left the area or what happened to her afterwards.

## The Wamble Family

**Gladys Brotherton, about 1918.**

Gladys moved from Starbuck to Walla Walla as a young woman in order to find work to support herself. On December 2, 1920, she married Clifton Wicks Wamble, who was born in Monroe County, Mississippi, on May 5, 1899. Wicks Wamble was an employee of the OWR&N. His World War I draft registration was filed in Starbuck on September 12, 1918, shortly before the armistice. However, he was back in Mississippi for the 1920 census, living with his parents, so it appears he did not serve in the military. By the end of that year he returned to Washington to marry Gladys in Walla Walla, where they lived for many years.

**Gladys at the farm in Starbuck.**

Gladys and Wicks had a daughter named Irene, born April 18, 1921, who sadly lived only a few hours. However, the couple was fortunate to have two more children: Nadine, always called "June," born June 21, 1922, and James Gordon, called "Jim," born July 21, 1924. Wicks died in Walla Walla on September 1, 1971 and Gladys on October 11, 1985.

Jim Wamble has remained in Walla Walla with his wife, Delpha May, whom he married on January 31, 1948. The Wambles knew the Joy family well and were aware of their half-cousin relationship, as were the Joys. With the Joy children's enrollment at Whitman College and with Harper's involvement with the school, there was and continues to be frequent interaction between the Wambles and the Joys.

**Gladys Brotherton Wamble, circa 1921.**

## John Lounsbury's Story

Soon after Irene's birth, John Lounsbury had disappeared from the scene. No record has been found of a divorce for him and Anna, but he did marry again in about 1900. In 1925, after much searching, Harper had the opportunity to meet his biological father, who was then living in Zeigler, Illinois, with his second

**John Cape Lounsbury, circa 1915.**

wife, Sally. John told Harper much of the family data that has been recorded here. They had a good time together – a pleasant experience for both of them.

Afterwards, in a letter to Henry and Annie Joy describing the meeting, Harper said, "John does not excuse himself … drink and lack of money coupled with his wanderlust were the reasons for his failure as a husband." He also told them he realized "I had only one father and mother and neither of them lived in Zeigler, Illinois. John had lost a son, but I had gained another father and mother through adoption. I'm not a Lounsbury – I'm a Joy – every bit of me – and I'm glad it's so." His letter brought well-deserved pleasure to the Joys. Their care and nurturing and strict upbringing helped make Harper Joy the man he became. John Lounsbury died October 19, 1925, not long after his meeting with Harper.

**Washington School, Ninth Street in Walla Walla, as it looks today.** *(Photo by Doris J. Woodward)*

## From School to Vaudeville

Harper and Irene were enrolled in the local Walla Walla schools. They first attended Baker School and later Washington School, a building that still stands in Walla Walla but now contains apartments. He and Irene made their way through the Walla Walla school system, as did their brother Harry. Very little is known about the early years when this family of five was living in Walla Walla. Their home was modest, but their family life appears to have been one of good humor, love and mutual respect.

In addition to school, Harper worked hard to help his parents with their home and yard. His one extracurricular pleasure was attending the nearest circus, to which he looked forward enthusiastically every year. Because of her stern religious beliefs, Annie felt the circus was not really acceptable entertainment, but she agreed to take the children each year so she could ascertain if the "devil had added any new features." To Harper, the circus visits were the highlight of his early life. He developed an affinity for the mysterious world of the big top. Harper loved "playing circus" in the backyard, even going so far as attempting to raise a big tent composed of burlap sacks. His *pièce de résistance* was his animal act, when he attempted to ride bareback on a cow. This feat did not appeal to the cow, however, and a sudden flip caused him to fall off, breaking an arm and putting his acrobatics on hold for a while.

Washington School, 8th grade graduation. Harper stands center stage, a forecast of his future life. Sister Irene is standing 2nd to his left.

For many years Harper was a member of the choir at the Methodist Church in Walla Walla

Henry and Annie Joy with Irene and Harper, grade school graduation, 1910.

Going to the circuses were glorious days for Harper. Looking back, it was perhaps not only the circus that caught his interest. He also loved the thought of performing before a live audience and hearing the laughter. He had the "bug," and it was a never-ending factor in his life.

When Harper entered high school, he found interests in other entertainment activities, such as the school band. He played both the baritone and the drums. He sang in the glee club and in 1912 also performed in the operetta "Priscilla." There is every indication his high school years were a pleasure. He was outgoing and made friends easily, attributes that benefited him throughout his life. He enjoyed campouts with a YMCA group, which was led by director F. D. Applegate, whom Harper later referred to as "Walla Walla's Father Flanagan." He never lost contact with Applegate, who felt Harper was "one of the most exceptional men he knew." He was certainly one of the most prolific and humorous of Harper's correspondents over many years. In 1947, Harper presided over a banquet at Walla Walla in honor of Applegate and his many years of service to the YMCA.

As graduation approached, Harper's senior picture was taken – it reveals a handsome, well-dressed young man. However, he did not graduate. The "smell of the greasepaint and the roar of the crowd" were luring him to the vaudeville stage. It happened on a Sunday while Henry and Annie were at church. Harper packed up his theatrical make-up and his various outfits and left home, telling sister Irene that he was going to Spokane to try his luck performing at the Spokane Theatre, the city's premiere vaudeville venue at the time. When the Joys returned from church, Harper was gone. Their reaction to his departure is not known, but since he was always a thoughtful and loving son, he stayed in contact with them frequently as he embarked on a lengthy tour of the vaudeville circuit. Performing was simply an enticement he was unable to resist.

**Harper's senior class picture, 1914, just before he left for vaudeville.**

Although his career started slowly in the Spokane area, it was not long before Harper was touring all over the United States with the Orpheum and Keith vaudeville circuits. He sometimes worked alone and sometimes teamed up with other vaudevillians to enhance his act. The duo of "Palmer and Joy" performed in San Francisco and other West Coast spots, and "Joy, Fay and Jeffries" appeared throughout the Midwest and was booked at the Miles Theatre in Detroit in 1915.

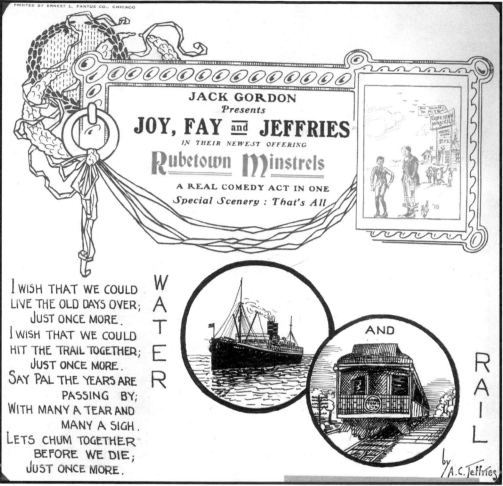

**Joy, Fay & Jeffries vaudeville poster – The "Rubetown Minstrels."**

This trio featured a rube/minstrel type of act, much of it performed in blackface. Harper's scrapbook from those days includes a page of stamp cancellations from many places, including New Mexico, Texas, California, Chicago, Detroit, Albany, New Orleans, Kansas City and various cities in the Northwest. These stamps probably came from letters he had written home, indicating he kept in close touch with Henry, Annie and Irene.

In a letter written in 1922, Harper described his experiences in "the show business" as follows: "(I was) employed as a business agent for the H. W. Campbell shows, as an advance agent for Hamilton's Minstrels and later as a performer on the Keith Circuit in the east and south." Of interest, Harper always referred to it as "the show business," which is actually the correct terminology.

There is a picture of him taken in New York City in 1917 and one of his brother, Harry, also taken there. Was Harry visiting him in New York? We cannot know, but it is pleasant to consider that these two brothers by adoption were good

**Harper's first vaudeville routines.**

**Harper Joy, New York City, 1917-1918.**

**Irene at the time of her marriage in California.**

**Harry Hess Joy, New York City, 1917-1918.**

## IRENE JOY

Irene attended college with financial assistance from Harper. After graduation, she moved to Fresno, California, where she was a teacher in the public
schools. Irene married Sten Odmann about 1930 and the couple had one
son, Stanley Joy Odmann, born December 28, 1932. Stanley was a member
of the San Francisco Police Department, in the Helicopter and Motorcycle
Patrol Division. He married Anne Richardson on December 4, 1971. Stanley and Anne had no children of their own, but she had several from a previous marriage.

Irene later married Dan MacIntosh, and the couple lived in San Francisco.
Irene died on September 18, 1952, at the age of 57. Her death was a real loss
to Harper, as the two had been very close and were frequently in contact.

**Irene Joy as a school girl in
Walla Walla.**

friends as they approached adulthood. Both pictures show them as good looking and self-assured adults.

Harper was living the vaudeville dream at the end of its heyday – although it continued spasmodically for years after. Its death knell was being sounded by the movie camera and the radio microphone. Perhaps Harper realized this, as he was an intelligent man. Maybe he just became tired of the traveling, but, as usual for Harper, he was always just a little bit ahead of the game. It was time for him to go home and move on with his life.

Harper returned to the home of Henry and Annie Joy in 1917. By this time, Harry and Irene had both left the Joy home, so Harper's parents were delighted to have him home again. He later said that it wasn't easy to forget those happy days on the road and come home to a small town. He wrote: "I sometimes wondered why I did it, but I suppose it was my loyalty to Mother Joy." Work was a necessity, and he was offered a job at the Union Pacific Railroad by Dave Broughel, a man who "gave me a lift when I needed it." Working for the railroad instilled in him a love of railroading that became evident again much later in his life.

Reflecting upon his vaudeville years, nothing about them was a waste of time for Harper Joy. While they may not have been financially rewarding, he certainly earned his way, and more importantly, he proved himself capable of entertaining, selling himself to a crowd of people and loving every minute of it. It was the portent of things to come.

Sometime during Harper's early years, he had an accident. He lost part of all the fingers of his left hand, leaving only the first joints and, fortunately, his thumb. According to his wife many years later, the accident occurred when he was working in a sawmill. The date is not known, but in a postcard from Olympia, Washington, dated January 13, 1915, Harper wrote to his parents: "My claim will only be about $700 … it could be much worse." This claim may have been a result of his accident; if so, the accident must have occurred after he left Walla Walla for vaudeville. He recovered and made the best of the situation, but it was something he never talked about in later life, although his son Ed recalls his father never wanted the children to use power tools.

Drifting along in an uninspiring job was not for Harper Joy. In 1918 Elsie Bowen, a friend of his mother, told Harper she believed he was the kind of man who ought to go to college. Annie Joy, who also undoubtedly felt Harper was fit for higher education, approved of her friend's advice, and Harper accepted it as a viable alternative to being a railroad clerk. The next phase of Harper's life was about to begin.

## Act Two:
## WHITMAN COLLEGE AND BEYOND

The establishment of Whitman College has an interesting history. It was the dream of the Rev. Cushing Eells to establish a school in honor of Marcus Whitman who, with his wife, Narcissa, had been killed in 1847 at the site of Waiilatpu, just six miles from Walla Walla. The development of the college, beginning in 1859 as the Whitman Seminary, experienced many setbacks until, in 1883, it was recognized as Whitman College, offering a four-year curriculum. By the time Harper Joy enrolled, it was a well-known institution respected throughout the Northwest.

Harper entered Whitman College in 1918, as World War I was coming to a close. Prior to that he had signed up for the draft but was declined because of the injury to his hand. On his registration card, he is described as tall, with brown hair and brown eyes, and he signed his name as "James Harper Joy." Since a military stint was out, the idea of entering college was even more tempting, and Harper accepted the challenge with enthusiasm, even though he was several years older than most of the others in his freshman class.

Since the Joys had no extra funds for higher education, Harper continued working during his college years. He was able to meet and exceed expenses by continuing to work for the Union Pacific and taking on other jobs as well. One of these was doing janitorial work at Falkenberg's Jewelers, who were so impressed with Harper they remained in touch with him for many years, always recommending him highly. He later wrote that during his first three years at Whitman he saved $4,500, at the same time contributing money to his parents and helping sister Irene through college.

The fact that Harper was older than most of his fellow students seemed to be a bonus. Whether true or not, he certainly made the most of his opportunities. He soon joined Phi Delta Theta, one of the major national Greek fraternities and also at the time one of the foremost men's social fraternities at Whitman College. It was his good fortune that many of his fraternity brothers during those college years were outstanding young men. Phi Delta Theta produced a number of exceptional graduates, which included not only Harper but also George Ingraham, Ralph Cordiner, George Yancey and Don Sherwood. All of these men started out as "poor boys" and became exceptionally successful in their careers.

**Science building, Whitman College campus in Walla Walla, about 1918.**

Don Sherwood's résumé is impressive. He became the chairman of the board of Sherwood & Roberts, Inc., president of the Walla Walla Canning Company, publisher of the *Walla Walla Union Bulletin*, and chairman of the board of American Sign & Indicator Corporation. Ralph Cordiner became chairman of the board of the General Electric Company in New York. George Yancey founded the investment firm of Murphey-Favre in Spokane. George Ingraham and Harper both had exceptional life-long careers as bond and securities salesmen. Harper's other accomplishments will be forthcoming. If *quality* attracts *quality*, the 1922 class of Phi Delta Theta at Whitman College is a good illustration.

## College Activities

During Harper's college years, Whitman was the home of another soon-to-be-famous student, William O. Douglas, class of 1920, future justice of the United States Supreme Court. In his book *The Early Years: Go East, Young Man,* Douglas includes an interesting segment about Harper Joy. Douglas had to work at an early morning janitorial job at Falkenberg's Jewelers to earn enough money to go to school, a job he shared with Harper Joy. Nothing can improve on Douglas's own description:

> I shared the janitor job with another student named Harper Joy. Harp had been in vaudeville with a "black-face" act ... Harp had stage presence and real ability. I think his musical scores of old-time vaudeville songs are one of our best collections, even to this day [1974]. Harp was the spark plug that brought the Whitman Glee Club to a new high. The singing was excellent, and Harp and his cohorts filled in with vaudeville acts between musical renditions. He played the role of Madame Zenda, who, though

**Hall of Music, Whitman College in 1918, when Harper enrolled there at the close of World War I.**

blindfolded, knew all and saw all. A sidekick worked through the audience, holding up a lady's scarf, a man's wristwatch, and the like. "What do I have in my hand, Madame Zenda?" always brought the correct response. What the clues were I never knew.

Douglas also reveals a somewhat embarrassing incident later in Harper's college career:

Harp and his Glee Club went on a successful tour, their last performance being in Spokane. The group included my brother Arthur, who by then was also a student at Whitman. They returned to Walla Walla by train and filled an entire Pullman car, except for one lower berth ... sold to an elderly couple. When Harp's crew took over the car, someone produced whiskey, and soon all hell broke loose. ... No one slept that night [and the unhappy elderly couple let the authorities know about it].

The result of this frivolity brought the wrath of Whitman President Stephen B. L. Penrose down on Harper, and he and the others were expelled from college. Harper asked for a hearing before the board of trustees. It would be fascinating to know what Harper said to defend himself. Undoubtedly he did an eloquent job of it, as he and the others were reinstated and he remained a good friend of President Penrose, later receiving excellent references from him. It appears Harper was one of the merry-makers that night, although there is no indication alcohol was ever a problem in his life. His worst offense was probably that, as the oldest one of the group, he should have been more responsible in overseeing the actions of the other students.

Douglas's description of Harper's connection with the glee club is important. Their performances throughout the Northwest during those years were exceptional, thanks in great part to Harper's contribution. Among the members of the chorus and orchestra, Harper and his pal Herbert Thompson were listed as impersonators and, besides "Madame Zenda," presented other humorous skits, undoubtedly a legacy of Harper's vaudeville years. In his memoirs, Douglas also recalled that Harper often sang during their early morning janitorial chores, usually old-time vaudeville songs. It was difficult to keep Harper Joy from performing under any circumstances.

Of equal importance to Harper's development was the debate team, which experienced frequent success in their matches with other colleges. Debate was highly regarded on college campuses in those years, and Harper and friend Ralph Cordiner competed with skill. Both men were members of Delta Sigma Rho, the national honorary debating fraternity. Harper's final commendation at Whitman came with the Award of Honors in his senior year, when he received the Commencement Marshalship.

Harper was also president of the student body, business manager of *The Pioneer*, the junior class annual, and confirming his entrepreneurial abilities, manager of "Harper's Bazaar," the canteen/concession stand at the YMCA. He hired a couple of other students to do the work.

If Harper's college years included any romance, we are to be left in the dark. If he ever honored a pretty coed with his Phi Delt pin, it was never recorded.

**Phi Delta Theta house at Whitman College, the home of some of Whitman's most illustrious students.**

**Whitman Glee Club. Harper is in the middle row, first on the left. Although Harper was able to sing and play several instruments, most of his performances with the glee club were as a comic entertainer.**

Maybe he was just too busy or maybe he preferred to remain silent for a reason! Nat Penrose, the son of Whitman's president and a good friend of Harper's, wrote a poem soon after graduation describing the romantic plights of some of their fraternity brothers. Harper enjoyed it enough to save it in his scrapbook:

> *First it was Wes who left us,*
> *Hooked by his little Anne*
> *Then the call of the wild got Ingraham,*
> *That social hound of a man.*
> *But the news of the fall of Baldy*
> *Came like a blow to our pride.*
> *There seems nothing else for a person to do*
> *But to rush out and grab him a bride.*

*But my faith in the gang of good fellows,*
*The best I have known since a boy,*
*May be shaken but never surrendered*
*If single remains Harper Joy.*
*He is the bachelor's by-word,*
*The hope of the single and brave.*
*If he falls – oh, to Hell with the women –*
*Then I'll surely be glad for the grave.*

- Nat Penrose

(The poem refers to Wes Mendenhall, George Ingraham and "Baldy," George Yancey)

With graduation over, Harper was ready to begin a career. He was almost 28 years old. It was time once again to try something new and become more stable. His YMCA friend, F. D. Applegate, offered him a job in Walla Walla starting in the fall, but Harper needed to find something to do over the summer. Once again lady luck smiled on Harper Joy.

**"Harper's Bazaar," a concession stand at the YMCA, one of the ways by which Harper earned money for college. Harper is in the center with an employee behind the bar and a customer seated at the table.**

**Whitman debate team. Harper is in the front row on the left. Ralph Cordiner is in the middle of the back row. Debate provided Harper with the skills he was later to use in speaking to numerous clubs and organizations.**

## Spokane and Ferris & Hardgrove

There was a job available in Spokane at the Pacific Fruit and Produce Company, to begin in August but, still hoping to find something that would start immediately, Harper contacted Joel E. Ferris, who was the president of the investment firm of Ferris & Hardgrove. He may have had an introduction to Ferris via mutual friends at Walla Walla or they may have met through Phi Delta Theta, as Ferris was also a member of the fraternity at the University of Illinois, class of 1895. Whatever the circumstances, Ferris was impressed with the young Whitman graduate and asked him to submit a formal letter of application. Harper's handwritten letter is a personal and modest résumé of his life and college experiences, and he includes an impressive list of references, many of them from former employers in Walla Walla.

A sampling of the originals, which have been preserved in one of the bound volumes of letters Harper saved throughout the years, read as follows:

> A. M. Jensen Co., Walla Walla:
> ... He seems to be a high class, straight-forward and highly educated young man with an excellent personality and a great gift of oratory.

Walla Walla *Bulletin:*
... His character is first class ... Believe that if you take Harper on he will meet your highest expectations in every respect ... He is one of the most promising young men sent out of Whitman for many years.

Farmers & Merchants Bank, Walla Walla:
I have a very high regard for Mr. Joy's ability ... He is endowed with a peculiar ability of meeting people and is full of energy and as far as I can determine has excellent business judgment. I have had a high regard for his character and habits throughout his college career.

Stephen B. L. Penrose, president of Whitman College:
I have a very high opinion of Mr. Harper Joy ... His habits are good, and his character is reliable. I believe that you will be justified in putting full confidence in him. I recommend him very heartily.

Baker-Langdon Orchard, Walla Walla:
... I think Joy is a very capable man, in that he knows how to get things done and do things himself ... He is a live wire, energetic, capable, original and thoroughly likeable ... he will do about twice the amount of rustling up business as the average employee.

The wisdom of these recommendations is astounding, as Harper soon proved them to be more than accurate.

Joel Ferris was convinced and hired Harper Joy as a bond and secuities salesman. It was to be Harper's first and also his last job, founded upon a relationship of respect and admiration between both men.

To consider that Harper Joy's career with Ferris & Hardgrove was just pure luck would be unfair and misleading. Harper undoubtedly made his own success. In those days, convincing people to invest in bonds and other securities was almost a door-to-door activity. Harper was good at this – he was a born salesman. Whether he was selling securities, himself, or his persona as a vaudeville entertainer, he was a personable guy, and people liked him.

**Joel E. Ferris, featuring the activities that interested him the most throughout his life, as financial tycoon, historian and, above all, gardener.** *(Cartoon by Sally Paine, now Sally Paine Pierone.)*

What was especially fortunate for Harper was the fact that Joel Ferris recognized the younger man's special abilities. Within two years Harper was sales manager for Ferris & Hardgrove. As an added asset, Joel Ferris gave Harper

# JOEL E. FERRIS

The man who became Harper Joy's employer and lifelong friend was one whose contributions to Spokane are exceptional. He was born in Carthage, Illinois, in 1874 and graduated from the University of Illinois. He studied law in Kansas City, Missouri, and later became involved there in banking and finance. In 1908 he moved to Spokane, working for the Union Trust Company, a joint affiliate of the Old National Bank and Traders National Bank. In 1913 he left Union Trust and founded the investment banking firm of Ferris & Hardgrove with George P. Hardgrove. In 1920 he joined the board of directors of the Spokane and Eastern Trust Company and in 1931 became its president.

On August 20, 1931, just before he assumed the job of president at S&E, Ferris wrote to Harper, revealing that it was a difficult decision for him and he would "need all the encouragement and sympathy from the men on whom I leaned so heavily, which means principally you." In reality, even in those difficult Depression years, he guided the bank to a growth of nearly five times its former size – a testimonial to his courage, vision and executive expertise. In 1936, when the Spokane and Eastern Trust Company merged with Seattle-First National Bank, Ferris was elected executive vice president.

Business was only a part of his life, however. He was actively involved during World War II in the bond drives, and later in the Hutton Settlement, Whitman College, Eastern Washington State College of Education, the Eastern Washington State Historical Society, the Friends of the Library at Washington State University; and, as a director, of the Davenport Hotel, the Interstate Telephone Company and the Spokane International Railway. Certainly of equal importance, Joel Ferris loved to garden, and his home and grounds were a testament to his expertise as a horticulturist.

When Joel Ferris died on December 14, 1960, the Spokane newspapers were full of articles praising him. His estate was valued at over $890,000, a large amount of which was given to his favorite local charities. His funeral services were held at St. John's Cathedral, officiated by the retired bishop, the Right Rev. Edward Cross, and the current bishop, the Right Rev. Russell S. Hubbard. Thirty pallbearers, many of them Spokane's foremost citizens, included Harper Joy.

In an article full of personal tributes, Harper Joy had this to say about his friend:

I started with him in this business in 1922, and had known him for nearly 39 years. Ours was a sort of father-son relationship. He was a great citizen. His judgment was sought by many. As one of Spokane's great pioneers, his loss is a severe one for the community.

Bishop Hubbard added these comments:

He was one of Spokane's most outstanding citizens, and he made a tremendous contribution to the development of the whole area. He was an immensely gracious friend, a man of sound judgment and one upon whom all who knew him depended a great deal.

The legacy of Joel E. Ferris is unique and honorable in Spokane's history. The Joel E. Ferris Foundation has provided funds for numerous worthwhile civic projects, and Ferris High School continues to honor the man for whom it was named. Closest to his heart would be the Joel E. Ferris Research Library and Archives at the Eastern Washington State Historical Society, Northwest Museum of Arts & Culture in Spokane, which houses his books, historic documents and personal papers. Harper Joy was certainly indebted to his kind and generous mentor.

**Ferris & Hardgrove. Front Row: Harper Joy, Joel E. Ferris; Back Row: Sam Whittemore, George Ingraham, Earl Dusenbery.**

the leeway to pursue the many interests that were to arise in his life in Spokane. One cannot minimize that contribution by Ferris. Instead of the corporate "mindset" so prevalent today, Harper was always able to contribute his abilities in many other fields, thanks to the support of Joel Ferris. In later years, Joel Ferris wrote to Harper: "Each year that passes I discover another enjoyable side to your character." Theirs was truly an association of mutual admiration.

According to the Spokane city directories of 1923 and 1924, Harper lived at the YMCA. In 1925 and 1926 his residence is given as South 623 Howard. Not too long after Harper's introduction to the Spokane business scene he became romantically interested in the woman who was to become of great importance in his future and in his life – Dorothy Mendenhall. Dorothy was not a stranger to Harper. She was the younger sister of two of his Phi Delt fraternity brothers, Wes and Hallam Mendenhall. The Mendenhalls lived in Walla Walla for a time, and Dorothy had attended and graduated from Walla Walla High School, but was too young at the time for a sophisticated "older" college man.

By 1922, when Harper arrived in Spokane, the Mendenhalls were living in Deer Park, and Harper often visited them, getting a good dinner and a place to sleep. "Little Dorothy" had grown into an attractive and appealing young woman. She was always known as "Dar" to her family, and so she became "Dar" to Harper as well. Never one to overlook a good opportunity, Harper began to court Dorothy, and it proved to be another one

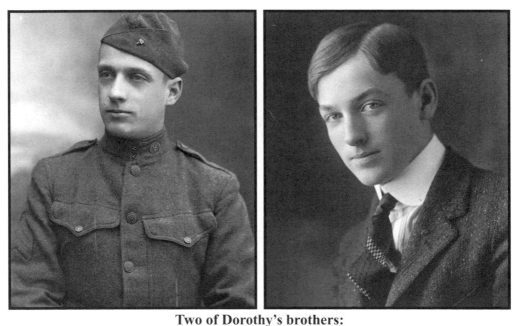

**Two of Dorothy's brothers:**

**James Wesley "Wes" Mendenhall**          **Hallam "Dick" Mendenhall**

of his most fortunate decisions. She was a woman of intellect and charm, and she proved to be a helpmate and support to Harper for the remainder of his life. She also, with the Brooks and Mendenhalls, provided Harper for the first time in his life with an extended family.

In 1925, at the urging of Joel Ferris, Harper traveled to Europe, the first of many such trips for him. His scrapbook includes innumerable pictures of foreign places, and it was an interesting and stimulating experience for him. Not surprisingly, he did some entertaining along the way. On Monday evening, September 7, 1925, aboard the White Star Line's RMS *Majestic*, the name of Mr. Harper Joy is included on a concert program held in the Dining Saloon [*sic*], where he regaled the audience with some "Rural Characterizations."

However, by the time he returned to Spokane he was ready to settle down. Harper purchased the house on Twenty-first Avenue and, on June 20, 1926, he and Dorothy were married in Deer Park. Of special interest, the man who married them was Stephen B. L. Penrose, the president of Whitman College, which speaks volumes about his opinion of Harper Joy and the Mendenhalls. The couple spent their honeymoon in Alaska, and on their return moved into the house that was to be their home for the rest of their lives.

**While Harper was in Europe, Dorothy was attending the Portland Art School. At the school costume party pictured above, she is the 2nd from the left in the middle row. Prophetic of things to come, she is dressed as a clown!**

**Harper and Dorothy on their wedding day, June 20, 1926, at her parents' home in Deer Park. She later admitted that they both had to laugh during the ceremony because she kept stepping on her veil.**

# Intermission

## THE BROOK AND MENDENHALL FAMILIES

## Henry Brook and Family

Dorothy Mendenhall's background is also significant to Spokane history. Her grandfather, Henry Brook, arrived in Spokane in 1883 and became involved in construction and the founding of the Washington Brick, Lime and Manufacturing Company (see sidebar). He and Kezia Letch were married about 1867 in England. A few years later they came to America with their first daughter, Mary, and settled in Anoka, Minnesota, where Henry was a young and ardent Methodist minister. The couple had four more daughters, one born in England and the other three born in Minnesota. Henry began to have trouble with his voice and felt that he would no longer be able to carry out his duties as a minister. As was fairly common in the post-Civil War days, the lure of the West was hard to resist, and Henry traveled to Spokane to investigate the economic possibilities.

Since it was to his liking, he found a home for his family, and later in the year, Kezia and their five daughters left Minnesota, traveling on one of the first Northern Pacific passenger trains, part of an excursion group of five that carried persons who had witnessed the "Golden Spike" celebration, marking the completion of the east and west lines of the railroad, where they joined at Gold Creek, Montana. In the *Spokane Chronicle*, July 29, 1964, the obituary of sec-

ond daughter, Helen Brook Mendenhall, describes the trip, which ended right in front of the home Henry had built for the family, located on the Northern Pacific tracks. It was later moved to the site of the future Spokane Hotel. Henry Brook soon built a large family home at the corner of Fifth Avenue and Wall Street (then called Mill). From an upstairs bedroom of that house, the Brook girls watched, in August of 1889, as fire swept through Spokane, destroying the entire downtown area of the young city. Following the fire, Henry's company was well equipped to furnish bricks and other clay products so desperately needed for the rebuilding of the city.

**Dorothy Mendenhall, 1925.**

**Henry Brook, born November 12, 1842 in Chelmsford, Essex, the son of Henry and Charlotte (Whitaker) Brook.**

After several moves, Henry and Kezia settled in a home at 1023 West Sixth, which still stands. They are listed there in the 1903 *Spokane City Directory.* Sadly, at that time there were now only four daughters. In a tragic boating accident on July 19, 1899, the youngest girl, Charlotte or "Lottie," drowned in Spirit Lake, Idaho, as did her longtime friend, Dottie Porter. Three other occupants of the rowboat managed to survive. The five young people were part of a large group of campers who had been spending a few days at Brickell Island. At the time of her death, Lottie was 21 years old and the only one of the five Brook girls still single. The other daughters had married in the intervening years.

Henry Brook died on January 16, 1908. He and Kezia were aboard the steamship *Roanoke*, on their way from Portland to California. Henry had been in failing health and it was hoped that the trip would prove beneficial, but it was not to be. His funeral was held in Spokane on January 20th, with three local Methodist ministers officiating. The pallbearers were S. Heath, D. B. Fotheringham, Judge W. A. Huneke, M. S. Bentley, George Hill, J. A. Havighorst, John W. Graham and E. J. Bower, all renowned Spokane businessmen and old friends. He was buried at Fairmount Cemetery (later to be called Fairmount Memorial Park) in a section that became the final resting place for many members of the Brook, Mendenhall and Joy families. His widow, Kezia, died a few months later and was buried on May 9, 1908 in the same plot.

**Kezia Letch Brook, born October 19, 1845 in Orsett, Essex, the daughter of William and Eliza (Wordley) Letch.**

### The Brook Children

1. Mary E., born in England in 1869; married James E. Daniels. Coming to Spokane from Wisconsin in 1887, Daniels was employed by Henry Brook, becoming superintendent of the Washington Brick, Lime & Manufacturing Company. In 1897, he became the customs collector for the Port of Spokane, a job he held for 34 years. The couple lived in Northport, Washington, and apparently had no children.

**The Brook Sisters, 1893. Back row: Nell and Alice; Middle row: Kate and Mary; Front: Lottie.**

2. Helen or "Nell," born in Minnesota on July 21, 1871; married Mark Francis Mendenhall of Spokane. They were the parents of six children, one of whom, Dorothy, married Harper Joy. More information about this family follows.

3. Alice M., born in England in 1874. The Brooks returned to England after Nell was born, probably to visit their families, and Alice was born during their vacation. The return trip was aboard the steamer *France*, which left London and LeHavre for New York on June 1, 1874. On the passenger manifesto, Alice is listed as an infant. She married Joseph M. Moore, an Internal Revenue Service agent, and they later lived in Tacoma. Their children were Josephine M. and Alice M.

4. Kate, born in 1875 in Minnesota; married William S. McCrea, who came to Spokane in 1888, became a real estate and insurance agent and eventually a

director of the Spokane & Eastern Bank. McCrea was involved with Harper Joy in various civic activities. Their children were Katharine, Mary Helen and William Jr.

5. Charlotte or "Lottie," born in 1878; died July 19, 1899.

Henry, born about 1885; died July 1889 of typhoid fever. He and his sister Lottie are both buried in the Brook plot at Fairmount Cemetery, the first of the family to be buried there.

Henry Brook,
age two.

## The Mendenhall Family

Nell Brook, the second daughter, married Mark Francis Mendenhall on January 31, 1893. He was born July 7, 1862, in Millerstown, Pennsylvania, the son of H. S. and Anna B. F. Mendenhall. In the 1790 census of Shamakin, Pennsylvania, H. S. Mendenhall is listed as a minister. Mark Francis later studied law and was admitted to the bar in Blair County, Pennsylvania. He came to Spokane in 1889 and taught in the old Spokane High School before he went into law practice with Judge W. A. Huneke, later with W. W. Tolman, and after that with V. T. Tustin. Mendenhall taught criminal law and torts for the Spokane Law School, a department of the newly created University of Spokane Falls, and in 1893 served as an officer of the Board of Education. He was a man of many interests and was instrumental in starting the Spokane Savings and Loan Society. He was the president of the Spokane Canal Company, at which time the company secured the water and storage rights at Newman Lake. He and Nell later moved to Deer Park where, as owner of the Mount Spokane Power Company, his office was located.

Mark Francis Mendenhall,
1893.

In the 1920 census, the family was living in Walla Walla, where Mark was listed as an attorney. Their two older sons were attending Whitman College and became acquainted with Harper Joy. At this time, daughter Dorothy was attending Walla Walla High School. By 1930 Mark and Nell were living in Seattle, where he was an attorney for a public utility company. Mark died January 28, 1941, at Virginia Mason Hospital in Seattle. He was buried on January 30th at Fairmount Cemetery. Nell remained in Spokane for many years after her husband's death, living to the age of 93. She lived at Rockwood Manor during her later years and died in July 1964. She had led a

**Helen "Nell" Brook Mendenhall, 1893**

full and interesting life, and was adored by her children and grandchildren, who called her "Grand Nell." She was noted for her artistic ability in various mediums and also enjoyed travel, making three trips to Europe as well as many to Mexico, Hawaii and Alaska. The Joy scrapbooks have several examples of this grandmother's artistic efforts. She sent the children letters written as rebus puzzles, which they had to translate. The letters are charming.

**One of Grand Nell's messages to the children – this one to Jimmy.**

## The Mendenhall Children

1. Mark F., Jr., born February 27, 1897; died in Seattle October 21, 1983, and is buried at Fairmount Cemetery.

**Mendenhall children: Mark, Wes, Dick and Dorothy.**

**Mendenhall men: Mark Sr., Mark Jr., Wesley, Dick and Gene.**

**Mark Mendenhall Jr.**       **Gene Mendenhall**       **Nell Mendenhall**

**The Mendenhall family at their home in Spokane on Seventh and Monroe.
Left to right: Dorothy, Dick, Mark Sr., Helen, Gene, Wes, Nell and Mark Jr.**

2. James Wesley or "Wes," born June 28, 1898; died June 24, 1995, in Portola Valley, California.

3. Hallam E. or "Dick," born March 20, 1900; died April 7, 1993, in Somers Point, New Jersey.

4. Dorothy Ida, born February 3, 1902; died June 14, 1994, in Spokane, Washington, and is buried at Fairmount Cemetery.

5. G. Eugene or "Gene," born November 2, 1907; died August 6, 1987, in Redmond, Washington.

6. Helen, born May 2, 1912. She is living in Albuquerque, New Mexico, with her husband of 64 years, Jay Todd, Jr.

Dorothy Mendenhall Joy was an artist like her mother. She attended Whitman College in the class of '26 for several years, joining the Delta Delta Delta sorority. At that time she was unable to complete her education, as she was needed to assist her family at home. Years later, in 1973 at the age of 71, she attended Whitworth College in Spokane, receiving her Bachelor of Arts degree. She was a woman of determination, a trait she had in common with her husband.

# THE WASHINGTON BRICK, LIME & MANUFACTURING COMPANY

Henry Brook and the architect Henry Preusse came to Spokane about the same time. The first project for Preusse was drawing plans for the First National Bank building, and the following year Henry Brook superintended the brickwork. Upon completion of the FNB, this pair worked again on the Gonzaga College building, some of the time in the actual construction.

Most of the brick in the Spokane area at that time was being produced by J. T. Davie. In 1886 Davie and Brook joined forces, purchased 80 acres on Cannon Hill and moved the brickyard to that site. Brook had previously purchased 40 acres in the area. Davie made the brick and Brook was the contractor. It was a successful venture for both men and proved to be a fortuitous move for the city of Spokane, as the brickyard at Cannon Hill eventually became Cannon Hill Park, one of the city's loveliest, with a pond today that was originally the clay pit of the brickyard. In 1888 Davie sold out his interest to Henry Brook, including the land. In the years before the 1889 Spokane fire, the brick produced at Cannon Hill was used to build the Keats Block, the old Hyde Block and the original First Presbyterian Church building.

Within a short time, Henry Brook joined forces with J. H. Spear and founded the Washington Brick, Lime & Manufacturing Company In the 1893 *Spokane City Directory,* the company is listed with Henry Brook, president, and J. H. Spear, secretary/treasurer. The offices were located at the corner of Stevens and Railroad Lane. It was a prominent company on the Spokane scene for many years and produced brick and clay products of great beauty.

The clay works was located at Clayton, Washington, north of Spokane, and here they manufactured beautiful varieties of brick, some of which were used to build the Spokane County Courthouse. In addition, they produced firebrick of superior quality, which was used not only to fireproof the courthouse but also the smelters at Butte, Montana. The company's lime plant was located just north of the brick works and was called "Valley Brook White Lime." Their offices and warehouses were located on Stevens at the Northern Pacific track.

The high quality of all the products from this company was well known throughout Washington, Idaho and eastern Montana, where they were used in buildings at the University of Washington as well as construction sites in Portland, Butte, Anaconda and many other places. After Henry Brook's death, the company reverted to his partner, J. H. Spear. With various owners, the company remained in business for many more years.

By the time Henry Brook died in 1908, the land of the old brickyard was being transformed, and in the 1910 *City Directory* the name of Cannon Hill Park is listed for the first time, as it had become part of the Olmsted brothers' plans for the Spokane Park System. It is now one of the loveliest of Spokane's many beautiful parks.

**Cannon Hill Park at 18th Avenue and Lincoln Street, three blocks north of the Joy home. This pond used to be the clay pit for the brickyard. Henry Brook at one time owned all of the property where Cannon Hill Park is now located.** *(Bamonte photo)*

The Joy house in 1928 at 825 West Twenty-first Avenue. The sunroom has been vastly changed, but the three pine trees still can be found in the front corner of the property. The linden trees growing today in the parking strips on both Twenty-first and Lincoln were planted by Harper soon after his trip to Europe, where he was impressed with the beauty of the lindens in Germany.

## Act Three:
## THE JOY FAMILY OF SPOKANE

Harper's work with Ferris & Hardgrove continued to thrive, and the intensity of Harper's public life was about to escalate. Evidence of early Spokane's business entertainment is found in a letter from Guy Toombs, the assistant manager of the Davenport Hotel:

> *My dear Harper:*
> *I am enclosing a program of the Northern Conference of Hotel Greeters, to be held here on Friday and Saturday, May 21-22 [1926].*
> *I cannot tell you how happy all of us are that you are going to entertain us on Saturday evening at our official banquet.*
> *With kind personal regards, I am*
> *Sincerely yours,*
> *Guy Toombs*

Meanwhile Dorothy settled down to create a real home for herself and her energetic husband. Within two years they were thrilled with the birth of a beautiful daughter, Nancy Brook Joy, born on April 2, 1928. Nancy's birth marked the real beginning of the Joy family in Spokane.

Also in 1928 they found themselves in a neighborhood that was featured in Ripley's "Believe It or Not." The **Joy** family was living next door to the **Happy** family (John and Marjorie); down the street, at Twenty-first and Adams, was the **Saad** family (Paul and Ethel); and a couple of

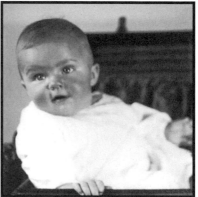

**Nancy Brook Joy, born April 2, 1928.**

blocks south was the **Gay** family (Nelson). Believe it or not!

## The Depression

The year 1929 and the beginning of the Depression brought new challenges to Ferris & Hardgrove, as well as to Harper Joy and everyone involved in the investment business. Times were tough, but Ferris & Hardgrove had always operated on a sound and conservative basis, and the crash was not the end of the world. They weathered the storm.

Always a cheerleader, Harper sent positive memos to his salesmen, who were understandably shell-shocked by recent events:

In November 1929, one month after the crash:
> ... we may well give thanks for a sales organization that doesn't quit, but changes its tasks to meet the new statistics. This "sitting-down" period is not for the "easy man" salesman in this business.

In March 1932:
> Give the next quarter a new point of view and it may be a winner for you ... what are you doing to attract business?

In May of the same year:
> As things are at present, it is not a matter of waiting ... it is rather of working ...The strong will survive ... the weak will be eliminated.

On March 31, 1933:
> It is very likely that we will look back on Monday, March 5th, when the President closed all of the banking institutions in the United States, as Black Monday of the Depression of the early '30s. I believe all of us feel that this will mark the bottom of the depression ... Let us continue the activity which has characterized our work during the period since the re-opening of the banks.

This was not Harper Joy, the clown. It was Harper Joy, the astute businessman.

The Depression also had its effect on Whitman College, which for several years had been having financial difficulties and now faced a drastic situation, a fact of life that plagued all state and private colleges during those years. Receiving little response from alumni to his plea for collecting delinquent subscriptions, President Penrose asked two young graduates for help – Harper Joy and Paul Garrett. It was the beginning of Harper's lifelong involvement with Whitman. He was forever dedicated to furthering the financial health of Whitman College, a place that was dear to his heart and enhanced by his energies.

For many of the details of the Joy family during these years, we are indebted to a marvelous collection of letters. Harper was a dedicated correspondent and, fortunately for his family, he kept the letters he received as well as carbon copies of his replies. This wonderful collection was put in a two-inch thick, hardbound book and contains a wealth of information and verbal picture of Harper Joy, the man. Other volumes were to follow. The letters, without exception, are informative and humorous, covering a wide variety of topics. Not only are Harper's letters humorous, those of his correspondents are as well. Reading them, page by page, convinces the reader that here was a man who was loved and admired. The letters come from a wide assortment of people–circus fans, investors, railroad magnates, Whitman graduates, Shriners and relatives–from all over the country. Harper was a "saver," and to make a researcher's job easier, he had all the letters bound in chronological order. What a luxury and treasure!

Many of them are truly moving. Just one example, from long-time correspondent Ross Beason, written December 18, 1934 from Miami Beach:

> Dear Harp:
>     Another year is almost gone. Without stilted phrases this is meant for a message of belief & friendship from me to you.
>     The years have been more pleasant because of you, Harp. Your sincere & sweet character & philosophy mean something to me and in my life. Believe this, old boy,
>     You are truly thrice blessed: (1) Dorothy, (2) The kids, (3) Your sane outlook.
>     Not just a greeting, Harp, but rather a weak effort to express what I feel.
>
>                                                             Your friend,   Ross

## Under the Big Top at Last

In spite of the Depression and all the financial ramifications of that event, the year 1929 was a memorable year for Harper for another reason as well. It

**Christmas party for Spokane orphans given by the Circus Fans of America, 1930. Left: Harry Goetz and James M. Doyle; In circle: Harper Joy and Joe Rupley; Right: Guy Toombs, Sam Whittemore and Roy Gill.**

marked his entrance into the circus world. The long ago dream of the young boy from Walla Walla was finally being realized. It began when Leonard Gross, a Chicago jewelry store liquidator, came to Spokane on business. He was known to Harper as an active member of the Circus Fans Association of America. Harper made a point of getting together with him to discuss their mutual love of the circus. The two men agreed to meet in Chicago the following spring and at that time drove 6,000 miles chasing circuses throughout the Midwest. Finally ending up in Moose Lake, Minnesota, with the Schell Brothers Circus, Harper made his circus debut, riding atop an elephant in the circus parade. If he hadn't been before, he was now "hooked." This was the beginning of long years of association with various circuses, when Harper spent two or three weeks each summer traveling with the big tops.

His friends were not silent on the subject of Harper's summers with the circus. One of the more humorous contributions is the following telegram from "Friar Tuck," otherwise known as George Yancey of Murphey-Favre and former Whitman classmate:

> *And now, ladies and gentlemen, you will have the enviable opportunity of seeing the world renowned benefactor of the human race, the great Harpist and Joyous bond salesman, the only one of his kind in existence. Step forward peepul and let him tell you how to live forever in blissful contentment with no cost except your entire wad. First come, first cleaned. No fooling, Harp, believe you chose the perfect vacation, and to make you doubly joyful we have started passing out corporate trust shares with a vengeance. The rest of the fellows here send their best and wish you a bagful of fun during your trouping.*
>
> *Always your friend,    Friar Tuck*

**Dorothy holding her second baby, "Jimmie" James Harper Joy II, born March 8, 1931.**

The circus years not only provided Harper with a couple of weeks of fun each summer, but also introduced him to a wonderful group of circus people who remained his friends and correspondents for the rest of his life. It also brought him into contact with the Circus Fans of America (CFA), an organization to which he contributed much of his enthusiasm in the oncoming years, eventually in 1933 becoming its president. The correspondence generated by his association with circus people and the CFA is interesting and often amusing.

On March 8, 1931, the Joys welcomed another baby into the family – son James Harper Joy II. Congratulations to the Joys often referred to the baby as "Harper Junior," but actually he was al-

**Benjamin Lounsbury
"Benny" Joy
born March 18, 1932.**

ways known as "Jimmie." Nancy now had a little brother to boss around, and Dorothy had her hands full with two small children. The following summer, Harper and Leonard were off again to enjoy the excitement of the big top on the West Coast and were invited to participate in the activities as clowns instead of just fans. Harper pulled several characters out of his repertoire – Mickey Mouse and the rollover balloon act, to mention just two. Ferris & Hardgrove continued to occupy Harper's daily existence, but the summer circuses were a clarion call that he couldn't resist. The Depression was in full swing in 1932, and life on the home front proved to be exciting as well. In March of that year, Harper discovered another talent, a role he surely never expected to play – that of "Dr. Joy." On March 18, 1932, second son, Benjamin Lounsbury Joy, was born at Deaconess Hospital, and in true Harper Joy fashion, he described it to friends in California: "Things happened in a hurry … and I didn't have a chance to get Dorothy to the delivery room. Everything worked out fine, however, and it's not too bad, in these depression times, to eliminate the cost of the delivery room, anaesthetic, etc. The doctor didn't arrive until it was all over, so I don't see how he can send me a bill for the usual $150."

That summer Harper was delighted to spend some time with the Al G. Barnes Circus. At one of the performances, musician Charlie Post introduced and con-

**Dorothy and Harper with three … no, four … elephants.**

**Circus Fans of America poster, 1933, showing Harper as the current president. He loved the CFA and found many lifelong friends among the members.**

**The wonderful faces of children at the circus.**

ducted a number he had composed, the "Harper Joy Triumphal March," in honor of the part-time clown who was now becoming something of a national celebrity.

One of the real pleasures that Harper experienced at the circuses was wandering among the spectators before the shows, paying special attention to the young boys who were looking on with longing, just as he had done as a boy. He always passed out free tickets to many of these young fans. His comment about this: "Those boys will never forget you as long as they live. If that isn't better than living on a church window pane, then I don't know immortality." Harper's dedication to circus life was not merely for personal gratification. For him, over and above the fun and the excitement, it was a calling.

The year Harper became president of the Circus Fans Association he wrote "A Few Thoughts for 1933" in the *CFA Journal*:

> Breathes there a man with soul so dead that the sight of the word CIRCUS will not give him a thrill? If so, I am sorry for him. There are some forms of public entertainment that are ephemeral; they have their day and cease to be. But the circus will never become obsolete, because there is in it a universal and eternal appeal. ... Ringling Brothers played our town many times and it was the great event of the late summer. From the time I entered the great tent until I emerged from it hours later, I was in Paradise. It was no illusion, no imaginary pleasure. ... As President of this Association I am extremely

anxious to have my regime characterized by harmony and good will – let's keep before us the Christmas spirit of unselfishness the year 'round. The Circus Fans Association is larger than any one of the members and no member should take it out on the organization merely because he does not approve of some individual in it, even if he be president. ... I do want your help in making 1933 a year of accomplishment and progress.

It was pure Harper Joy, and evidently his tenure as president of the CFA was very successful. The depression years passed with Harper continuing to spend his summer vacations on the road. When the circuses were in the Northwest, he had his family with him, and Dorothy and the children can be seen in frequent photographs atop elephants or with the clowns. In 1936 the Cole Brothers Circus was in Spokane – a special treat for all the Joys. And something else occurred that year. It was also a treat, but not only for the Joy family.

## The Cannon Hill & Pacific Railroad

When the children awoke on Christmas Day in 1936, a surprise had arrived upon the scene in the Joy's backyard at 825 West Twenty-first Avenue – a railroad by the name of the Cannon Hill & Pacific. It was to change the face of South Hill entertainment for children for 20 years. It was not a railroad as such. It didn't move and it consisted at first only of a locomotive, but it was a real locomotive and it stood on real railroad tracks. It was a "saddle back" steam engine, which had been built in Davenport, Iowa, in 1905. In its working days it was used for construction work on the Spokane Portland & Seattle Railway.

**The Cannon Hill & Pacific Railroad, Christmas Day, 1936. Ben as engineer, Dorothy, Harper, Miss Backlund, Nancy and Jim.**

**The Cannon Hill & Pacific pictured with its newly acquired caboose.**

It is not known just when Harper conceived the idea of providing a railroad for the pleasure of his children and the neighborhood children and, incidentally, for his own pleasure as well. He had worked for railroads early in his life, and his father, Henry Joy, was also a railroad man. Railroading was a very real part of his life, as it has been for so many who had close connections with railroads in their formative years. It is perhaps difficult for today's generation to realize the tremendous impact railroads had upon yesterday's children, but to those who remember the steam locomotives – their sound, their smell, and their magnificent size – they are memories never to be forgotten.

Harper's contribution to Spokane history with the CH&P is a monumental one. Countless numbers of today's Spokanites have fond memories of their youthful days, playing on the locomotive in the Joys' backyard. In later years, Harper had a caboose built to tag along after it, but both pieces were always stationary. Actually the locomotive was still a working steam engine, and Harper often fired it up, using it to burn unwanted paper.

Harper had a tremendous amount of fun with this new plaything. He created a timetable, with destinations such as Slippery Gulch, Joystown, Joysburg, Somewhere in France, and St. Joy. Also he printed some Rules of the Road:

• Train runs only during periods of total eclipses, tidal waves and days when security dealers are happy and contented.

• Passengers over 87, accompanied by their parents, are permitted to ride half-fare.

• "Shades of Casey Jones" – this train went away one day and never came back. We carry it on the time table for sentiment's sake.

• We never could figure it out, but whatever time this train starts it always arrives on Thursday.

• Users of cut plug tobacco are respectfully reminded of the idiosyncrasies and foibles of the fickle wind.

• Security salesmen must wear shirts and shoes in transit and must also ride in Jim Crow cars.

• Any passenger arriving at destination hill will be awarded the famed Cannon Hill & Pacific Croix de Guerre complete with kisses by a genuine French general in good repair.

• Any passenger refusing to get out and push on up grades will be frowned on by the management.

• Due to the fact that Spokane Ordinances require that all trains be preceded by a man on foot waving a red warning flag, the road cannot assume responsibility for injuries suffered when irate bulls remove the cars forcibly and violently from the tracks.

He had CH&P letterheads printed, which included a picture of the locomotive with sons Jim and Ben, and an impressive board of directors listed across the top:

R. Lewis Rutter, President; Joel E. Ferris, Financial Vice-President;
Louis M. Davenport, Dining Car Service
John E. Blair, General Counsel; Edward W. Robertson, Claim Agent
Jimmie Joy, Chief Engineer; Bennie Joy, Freight & Passenger Agent;
Harper Joy, Supt. Fuel Conservation

*"THE ROAD TO YESTERDAY*
*OUR ROAD NOT AS LONG, BUT JUST AS WIDE AS ANY"*

Over the years he issued passes for the CH&P, sending them to numerous railroad officials and other friends and people of importance across the country. That they enjoyed his sense of humor cannot be doubted, as witnessed by excerpts from some of their responses:

From Bill Gabriel of San Francisco, January 28, 1937:
> I simply refuse to be even as much as a little surprised as to anything that comes to me over your signature ... I have certainly come to the conclusion that nothing is quite beyond your capacity.

From the Washington Railroad Association, Richard McGough, March 22, 1945:
> Your most gracious act in sending me a pass on your road is greatly appreciated ... I esteem it a privilege to add the pass to those of the Chicago, Milwaukee, St. Paul & Pa-

cific; the Great Northern; Northern Pacific; CB&Q; Union Pacific; SP&S, etc., which I carry. ... Joe Drumheller tells me that the Cannon Hill & Pacific has approximately one block, or 1/12 of a mile of tracks in operation. Your dues [in our association] would come to approximately 1/60,000 of the estimated $12,000 annually, or, in rough figures $0.20 per year. Naturally these figures will vary from year to year. But we believe the annual costs of membership to your line will be exceeded by the benefits gained. ... We shall be glad to grant you the privilege of paying dues in semi-annual, quarterly or monthly installments.

## From the *New York Times*, Ward Allan Howe, December 10, 1945:

It is with a great deal of pleasure that I enter into the brotherhood of the Cannon Hill & Pacific Railroad via the pass which you so kindly sent. I appreciate it very much. While I cannot find the Cannon Hill & Pacific listed in the Class I roads (or even the Class II or III), I feel that it must be there somewhere, in spirit anyway. A visit to the "Heart of the Inland Empire" has long been on my schedule (this summer I got as far as Jackson Hole) and when I do make it, one of the first things on the agenda will be an inspection of the rolling stock of the CH&P.

## From the Spokane International Railroad Co., F. C. Rummel, February 7, 1949:

Thanks so much for the pass on the Cannon Hill & Pacific Railroad. In looking at the photograph of the engine, it would seem that it was ready for service. ... I will be glad to cooperate to the fullest extent in getting new business for the railroad.

## From the Great Northern Railway Company, John W. Budd, president, June 8, 1952:

Your kindness in sending the pass on the Cannon Hill & Pacific Railroad is very much appreciated. ... In the interest of friendly relations I am enclosing herewith a pass over the Great Northern for the year 1952 which I hope you will also be able to use.

## From the Milwaukee Company, Joseph T. Johnson, president, July 11, 1952:

I accept this pass subject to all of the conditions shown on the back and will, of course, do whatever I can to stimulate traffic over your line. I am not the least bit perturbed by the age of the two principal executives, as I have been watching the Republican Convention for the last few days. Nothing could be more childish than that.

Only one letter exists that was written on CH&P stationery. It is dated January 21, 1937, and is addressed to Dorothy M. Joy:

Dear Madam:

The Board of Directors of the Cannon Hill & Pacific Railroad had previously considered the placing of your name on its stationery as an officer of the company, but it was brought to the attention of the Board by Mr. Harper Joy, Superintendent of Fuel Conservation, that it would not be suitable to appoint you as Chairman of the Ventilating Committee, principally for the reason that it was stated that you were always opening doors and windows in the coldest sub-zero weather, and allowing the heat, which is produced at tremendous expense, to fly out the window and the cold air to rush in. We feel that anyone so addicted to letting all the warm air rush out the train windows would cause our patrons to abandon our lines and to use competitive lines.

Trusting that we have made ourselves clear and that you will appreciate our position in the matter, we are

> Very truly yours,
> /s/ Joe Doaks, Chairman Ventilating Committee

The Cannon Hill Road was sold to Spokane Metals in July 1956 after 20 years of service, and its last day was celebrated by a lengthy article and a picture in the Spokesman-Review. It was the end of an era on the South Hill.

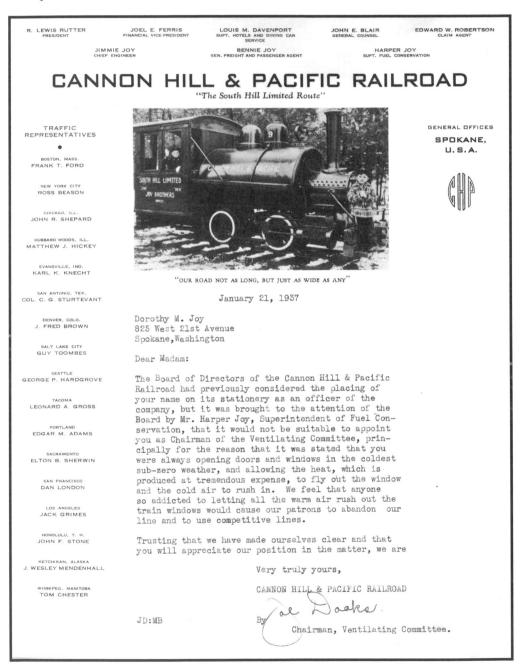

12   Wed., July 18, 1956.   The Spokesman-Review

## It's the Last Run for Cannon Hill Line

A group of youngsters enjoyed one last "ride" on the "South Hill Limited" yesterday morning. Harper Joy, investment firm executive, sold the Cannon Hill and Pacific railroad to Spokane Metals company. It was in Joy's back yard for 20 years.

## Joy's Cannon Hill Railroad Sold; Children Say Good-By

The shortest railroad in the Pacific Northwest, with only 60 feet of track, was "liquidated" in Spokane yesterday.

Locomotive No. 9 of the Cannon Hill and Pacific railroad took its last "ride" yesterday with a dozen youngsters aboard.

Equipment of the railroad, operated for 20 years in the back yard of the Harper Joy residence at W825 Twenty-first, was sold to Spokane Metals company.

Joy, executive vice president of Pacific Northwest company, investment firm, purchased the railroad in 1936 as a Christmas present for his children.

### Many "Passengers"

Over the years, hundreds of neighborhood youngsters have "traveled" on the line, known as the "road to yesterday" which was "not as long but just as wide as any."

The "saddle-back" locomotive was built at Davenport, Iowa, about 60 years ago and in 1905 it was used by a Spokane contractor for construction work on the Spokane, Portland and Seattle Railway company at Lyle, Wash.

When the kids heard the "South Hill Limited" was headed for the junk yard, they swarmed aboard for one last "ride."

Benjamin Endleman, president of Spokane Metals and new owner of the Cannon Hill and Pacific, plans to keep the train intact at his yards.

### Museum Piece

"It won't be destroyed," he said, "we just bought it as a museum piece."

Joy was superintendent of fuel conservation for the railroad. Other officials in past years were R. Lewis Rutter, president; Louis M. Davenport, superintendent of hotels and dining car service; and Joel Ferris, financial vice president.

Two Joy sons had important posts on the Cannon Hill and Pacific. James H. Joy was chief engineer and Benjamin L. Joy was general freight and passenger agent.

Joy, who once worked at the freight office of the Union Pacific Railroad company at Walla Walla, said he always has been interested in railroads.

## DRIVER HANDED 30 DAYS' JAIL

A 30-day jail sentence and $100 fine was ordered yesterday in police court for Floyd A. Byler, E1027 Gordon, charged with driving under the influence of liquor. His driver's license was suspended for six months.

Byler served oral notice of appeal and Judge Gorden S. Lower set bond at $500.

Fine of $25 each were levied against John F. Joslin, Fairchild air force base, charged with having no driver's license; Einar J. Ervig, N3014 Addison, red light violation, and Laurence C. Knorr, E4424 Frederick, loud muffler.

Bonds of $35 each were forfeited by Vernon L. Gray, N1309 Howard, charged with speeding 48 miles an hour; Donald C. Howard, E2714 Heroy, speeding 50 miles an hour, and Dan F. Primmer, Valleyford, Wash., speeding 40 miles an hour in a 20-mile zone.

A $30 bond was forfeited by Joyce A. Peone, E12020 Third, Opportunity, speeding 30 miles an hour in a 20-mile zone.

The *Spokesman-Review* announced the demise of the CH&P with a picture of neighborhood kids enjoying their last ride.

**The CH&P engine on its way to the Schaefer Lumber Yard in Lewiston.** *(Photo courtesy of the Inland Empire Railway Historical Society.)*

**The CH&P saddle tank as it stands today at the Interstate Fairgrounds in Spokane.** *(Photo by Doris J. Woodward.)*

## A 1957 letter Harper wrote to an old friend from his OWR&N and Union Pacific days, William L. Watters

"Over forty years ago I called the crew for OWR&N ... and met you for the first time then. You were such a nice guy. Perhaps you were just being kind to the kid from 9th and Pine [Walla Walla]. Life has been good to us, Bill. Your kindness and sympathetic understanding has created untold good will among the countless thousands who rode your trains on the Union Pacific. May I send you this last pass on the Cannon Hill & Pacific -- now gone to Railroad Heaven too. As one of your admiring friends of yesteryear may I wish for you a long and happy life in retirement, and say, "Well done, thou good and faithful servant!"

This was the final pass that Harper issued for the CH&P, but in 2006 the author received a pass of her own, issued by Ed Joy. I think perhaps this is the last one and was an honor to receive.

The old Cannon Hill & Pacific has not quite gone to "railroad heaven" yet, however. After leaving the Joy backyard, it was sent to Lewiston, Idaho, to be housed at the Shaefer Lumber Yard, where it was dismantled and stored for almost 40 years. Thanks to a group of intrepid and dedicated Spokane railroad enthusiasts with the Inland Empire Railroad Historical Society (IERHS), the grand old engine was brought back to Spokane and can be found at the society's present headquarters at the Interstate Fairgrounds. The saddle tank can be seen on an outdoor track, but the rest of the parts are in the process of being reassembled in the shop. Future plans of the IERHS include moving their entire operation to Reardan, Washington, where they hope to display more of their renovated locomotives, cars and memorabilia celebrating the history of the railroad in America. With luck, the Cannon Hill & Pacific will again blow its whistle and ring its bell and, perhaps, get up a head of steam for a trip down memory lane.

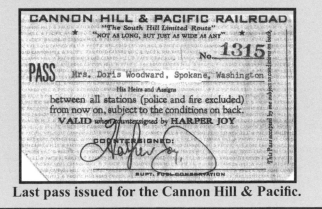

Last pass issued for the Cannon Hill & Pacific.

# Applause! Applause!

The years after the arrival of the CH&P and before the start of World War II were busy ones. Harper continued to spend at least three weeks each summer with one circus or another and was becoming famous because of it. His notoriety began with a brief note that went out on the news wires after a performance in Wenatchee. The flood began. The Associated Press wired Spokane for a story, and soon the *New York Times*, the *Milwaukee Journal*, the *Philadelphia Public Ledger,* the International News Service, the North American Newspaper Alliance and other papers and services followed suit. Most of the requests went direct to the offices of Ferris & Hardgrove. The papers and magazines loved printing stories about the "millionaire banker and clown." Harper arrived home to find himself somewhat of a celebrity with a national reputation. Many of the stories were absurd, such as one that drew the conclusion that, because of the Depression, Harper needed the second job to support his family. Others claimed it was a "release from the monotony of work." Needless to say, given Harper's sense of humor, he undoubtedly delighted in such erroneous reporting and psychoanalysis.

Harper was also no stranger to local show business. In the 1920s, he joined the University Club Players, who, in 1929, produced a silent movie entitled *Crown*

**Harper as a Russian interpretor and Joe Albi as Anastos Mikoyan, featured on KHQ-TV in 1959.**

*Jewels*. Although it was an amateur endeavor, it is a classic. Written and directed by Frank Davies, it featured a host of Spokane actors and actresses, including Mary Margaret Hawes as the leading lady, Harper Joy and John H. Happy. Harper and Mark Hawkins were the duo in the film that kept a thread of comedy running through the story. Dr. Frederick G. Sprowl was the head cameraman and, with his crew, managed several bits of trick photography.

Almost 40 years later, in April 1967, the film was resurrected and shown to a gathering of museum volunteers at the Cheney Cowles Memorial Museum Auditorium. Harper was the commentator for the evening and described how the University Players borrowed everything they could to make the film, including the Nell Shipman movie equipment that had been used when she made her films on location at the Playera Studio in Minnehaha Park. *Crown Jewels* also featured local Spokane scenery–Manito Park, Rimrock Drive, First Avenue and several buildings of interest. According to Harper, "It is a miracle we ever finished it."

Today *Crown Jewels* is in the custody of the Northwest Museum of Arts and Culture, and viewing the film is an interesting step back in time. Sadly, the quality of the film (now on DVD) is poor, but the period costumes, the acting and the stage settings are still a pleasure to see. One of the more fascinating aspects of the film as it concerns Harper Joy is the fact that the artist, A. Rutgers Van der Loeff, not only appears in it briefly, but all the cartoon-type artwork that begins each new scene was created by his talented hand. Van der Loeff became one of Harper's best friends, as evidenced by his connection with the Davenport Hotel later in this story.

As the years progressed, Harper was involved in many aspects of entertaining. He was frequently asked to appear at conventions and civic functions, sometimes as the after-dinner speaker, sometimes as an entertainer, and sometimes as both. An example of the appreciation people felt for his efforts is a note from George Haslett, president of the Navy League of America in Spokane, after an evening's entertainment: "Ten thousand thanks, Harp, for being our ring-master."

In 1937 he became the executive vice president of Ferris & Hardgrove, so there is no doubt his activities and blossoming fame were felt to be of benefit to the company. He also attended many national financial and CFA conventions, becoming well known by many people nationwide for activities beyond the circus performances. His was a familiar face people enjoyed seeing, and his contributions to the world of business and entertainment were received enthusiastically. Spokane finally had a favorite son who, along with fellow Spokanite Bing Crosby, was receiving national recognition.

During this period he joined the National Association of Securities Dealers, Inc., headquartered in Washington, D.C., and for many years was an active

# Scenes from the 1929 Silent Movie
## CROWN JEWELS

The following film clips from the 1929 silent film *Crown Jewels* are presented here to convey some essence of the humor and originality that are prevalent throughout the movie. Produced by members of the University Club, many of the names and businesses found below were well known in Spokane from the 1920s and can still be recognized today. This silent movie was produced by amateurs with the equipment available at the time, which unfortunately, does not compare to the technology available today. All drawings are by A. Rutgers Van der Loeff.

*Crown Jewels*

with

Mary Margaret Hawes

and

Franklin Greenough

The Chairman of the Entertainment Committee was trying to secure the permission of the President of the University Club to make a Moving Picture.

Charles Gillingham
Edwin D. Ham

"In addition to having actors the University Club has among its members—

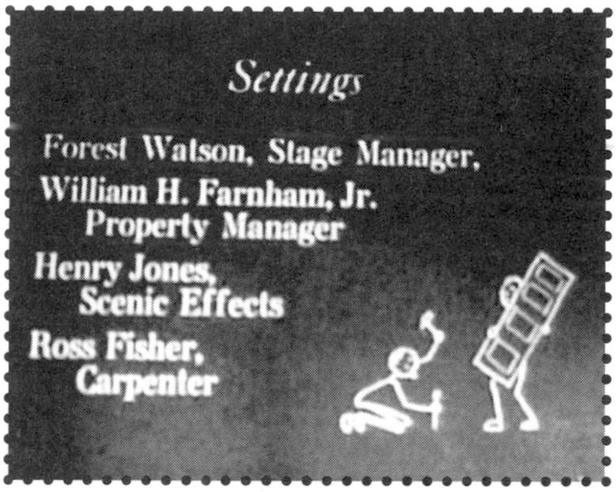

*Settings*

Forest Watson, Stage Manager,
William H. Farnham, Jr.
Property Manager
Henry Jones,
Scenic Effects
Ross Fisher,
Carpenter

*Titles*

Edited by Stoddard King
Illustrated by A. R. Van der Loeff

*Photography*

Dr. Fred G. Sprowl,
Head Photographer
Dr. C. B. Ward,
William H. Cowles, Jr.

**Electrical Effects**

Bernhard Olsen, Master Electrician
Donald S. Campbell
Matthew F. Murphy
Lester R. Gamble
Edward E. Scofield
A. H. Beckwith
J. E. E. Royer

**Technical Staff**

Frank Davies, Director

Katherine Chickering,
   Assistant Director

Margaret Paine,
   Technical Editor

Lilian Lane Kimble,
   Continuity Director

**Business Organization**

John G. Reinhardt,
   Production Manager

Joseph Rupley,
   Publicity Director

John H. Happy,
   Theatre Manager

**Dedication**

For only a nickel in the good old days they gave us thrilling Saturday afternoons and sleepless Saturday nights.—It is to the Motion Picture Producers of Years Ago: Biograph, Pathe, Keystone Selig, and all the rest, that this picture is affectionately dedicated

In this picture it is the woman who pays, because this picture is a slice of life as it is really lived—Life as it emerged from the Dark Ages and crept painfully toward Civilization, making all stops—Draw the curtain, Master Showman, make your puppets dance, and send the bill to —————

**Woman**

member of the group, eventually as vice-president and chairman of the Public and Member Relations Committee. Upon his retirement he received a letter of commendation from Wallace H. Fulton, the executive director of the association. Following is a brief excerpt from Mr. Fulton's enthusiastic comments:

> Your imprint will be for a long time on the NASD News, the Annual Report, and other literature which the Association sends out. We who have had the privilege of listening to your reports ... will miss them. They were high lights of our meetings. You put together a lot of good common sense, and some very good ideas in a very palatable and wholesome package. ... I know you stand ready to be of help when called upon.

Despite the newspaper stories, Harper Joy was hardly a millionaire. He never received any money for his circus performances, but the family was financially secure and in 1936 purchased property on nearby Liberty Lake. Looking back now, the children feel that buying the cottage was compensation from Harper to Dorothy for being so patient about the summer weeks when he was away "circusing." She loved the lake, as did the children; summers were a pleasure to anticipate through the long, cold winter months. Harper, too, enjoyed the lake place, and Liberty Lake was close enough to commute to Spokane during the

**Ready for a new Huckleberry Finn adventure, the "Sea Goon" and her crew: Jim Joy, unidentified boy, John Rademacher, Nancy and Ben Joy at the tiller. The sail (or bedsheet) is about to be hoisted. In later years, Jim was a Navy man during the Korean War. John Rademacher flew with the "Blue Angels" and served in the U.S. Navy during the Viet Nam War.**

**Press Club party at Liberty Lake. Harry Goetz, as "Dutch Jake," filled the job of bartender.**

**Ed and Linda Joy with the author at the Joy cottage at Liberty Lake, lakeside view.** *(Bamonte photos)*

**Liberty Lake looking east.**

Painting of "Harper the Clown," which hung for many years at the Davenport Hotel, was a gift to Louis Davenport from Harper. It now graces the wall of the Liberty Lake cottage next to the fireplace. The inscription in the lower right corner reads: "To my friend Louis M. Davenport in memory of old circus days in Pawnee City, Nebraska, Harper Joy."

A Christmas season greeting from the Joy family on permanent display in the Liberty Lake cottage.

week. The family still owns this comfortable, unpretentious cottage and continues to enjoy spending time there during the summer.

## Louis Davenport and the Circus Room

Another interesting aspect of Harper Joy's life during these years was his association with Louis Davenport. It is not known how these two men became friends, but it may have been through their mutual association with Joel Ferris. However it happened, Louis Davenport was intrigued by Harper's association with circuses and decided to honor Harper with a room at the Davenport Hotel to celebrate his friend's circus connections. The Circus Room was begun about 1935, when Louis hired a local sign painter, A. Rutgers Van der Loeff, to decorate Room 730 with a circus theme. Van der Loeff was actually much more than just a sign painter, and his work is excellent. It is the only room at the later-renovated hotel (2002) that was not changed and remains as it was originally decorated, except for an addition (deservedly so) of pictures of Walt and Karen Worthy, the owners who made the Davenport renovation possible.

The reason for the creation of the Circus Room is not known. Tom McArthur, the director of communications and historian for the Davenport Hotel, believes it was done as a surprise for Harper Joy, Louis Davenport's friend, when he returned from one of his summer sojourns under the big top. Tom feels that the Circus Room is Spokane's biggest inside joke, meaning that its humor and detail would have been understood by everyone for whom its understanding was intended, and for the others it would be merely a nicely decorated room.

The decorations include an around-the-room parade of circus pictures, calliopes, bandwagons, animals, acrobats and clowns. We are indebted to Tom McArthur for much of the following information. He has been interested in the history of the Circus Room since his arrival at the Davenport several years ago and has contributed many of the fascinating details printed here.

The parade begins at the right of the door when one is standing inside the room. The first person pictured is Fred Bradna, who spent 40 years as the equestrian director of the Ringling Brothers and Barnum & Bailey Circus. Bradna is regarded as the father of modern-day ringmasters. He was a tall, distinguished German, sporting a pencil-thin moustache, high black boots, bright red coat and silk top hat. He never once made an announcement, perhaps self-conscious about his thick German accent. Instead, he used his whistle to govern the progress of the entire show. The equestrian director was master of ceremonies and straight man for the clowns. Bradna and Joy would have worked closely together in the circus.

Second in the parade is Ella Bradna, Fred's wife and fellow circus performer who, according to legend, met Fred when her horse threw her during a performance, and she landed in her future husband's lap.

The circus wagon, adorned with furniture tacks and welding rods, was originally ornamented with various national flags, including those of Germany, Italy and Japan. Legend has it that when the United States entered World War II, Mr. Davenport secured a step stool and, with his pocketknife, personally removed the aforementioned flags, which were, at the time, the flags of the Axis powers. Legend further says that Louis proclaimed, "No enemy of my country shall be in my hotel!"

Of special note, when viewing the circus room, many of the gentlemen in the parade are holding up their right hands with the first and fourth fingers parted in the form of a "M." This apparently is a "sign of calling" within the Masonic order, to which there is a corresponding "sign of recognition." Of course, this is known only to Masons. Since Louis and Harper, as well as Van der Loeff, were all Masons, they would have known how to respond to the calling on the wall. (Note that one young man in the parade is shown attempting to learn the sign and may one day become a Mason.)

Other known individuals in the parade (on the north wall) are Buffalo Bill Cody and Aubrey White, the "father" of the Spokane park system and fellow member of the park board with Louis Davenport. Louis himself appears on the east wall, overlooking his restaurant. Near him are his wife and son, Verus and Lewis. They disliked having their pictures taken and are standing with their backs to the viewer, as they also appear on the opposite wall.

When one has gone completely around the room, in the corner just left of the door can be found a figure that is definitely Harper Joy, with hat cocked over one eye and cigar in mouth. Behind him stands a boy carrying a water pail in each hand. Surely this must be a depiction of the young Harper in Walla Walla, who was said to be "the best water carrier a circus elephant ever had!"

It is believed the entire circus parade was carved from a roll of gray cardboard, something that would have been available in a storeroom of the hotel and without any cost. According to the Davenport Hotel's present-day artist-in-residence, Melville Holmes, who restored the Circus Room for the Worthys in 2002, he has a great deal of admiration for the artist(s) who created the Circus Room. Their brushwork was "deliberate and confident, suggesting a well-rehearsed hand," according to Mr. Holmes.

The background "city" on the walls is unknown. The buildings are not tall and suggest a small town, certainly not the Spokane of the 1930s. Could it possibly represent Pawnee City, Nebraska, the city in which Harper Joy and Louis

Davenport shared memories of the circus? The beltline molding separating the striped wallpaper below and the circus pictures above is intentionally red, since the "reds" were the best seats at the circus. These were "real" seats, not bleachers, in the front of the tent.

During those years and for many more to come, Van der Loeff was a good friend to Harper and Dorothy Joy and annually assisted Harper in designing the Christmas cards the Joy family sent to their many friends. These Christmas cards are works of art and imagination and something that Harper and Van der Loeff collaborated on for many, many years. Ed Joy says that some 500 Christmas cards were sent out each year and, when he was old enough, he assisted in hand addressing them all.

The Christmas card project began simply enough with Harper sending them himself after his graduation from college. The development of the cards over the years is an indicator of the family's growth, beginning with Dorothy, and expanding with the birth of each child.

**Tom McArthur explains the artwork on the west wall of the Circus Room to Suzanne Bamonte and Doris Woodward.** *(Bamonte photo)*

**Fred Bradna, equestrian director, and wife Ella.**

**Elephants on parade with East Indian trainers**

**Driver in control of the lion's wagon**

**Circus wagon built around a world globe**

**Spectators watching the camels on parade**

**Russian cossacks on parade**

Louis Davenport
with son, Lewis, and wife, Verus

Japanese flag has lost its
"rising sun"

Spectator making the Masonic
"sign of calling"

Young boy striving to copy the
Masonic sign

Roman chariot being pulled
by zebras

Artist Van der Loeff working in the
Circus Room with an assistant

Harper Joy, as an adult, and
young Harper as a water carrier

The moustached man has not yet
been identified

Several spectators watching
the circus parade

The man on the left is Aubrey White,
the "father" of Spokane Parks

Spectators pictured with a mounted
American Indian in full headress

Newcomers to the Circus Room
walls: Walt & Karen Worthy

# A. RUTGERS VAN DER LOEFF
## Creator of the Circus Room

Abraham Rutgers Van der Loeff was born in Groningen, Holland, on November 17, 1882, the son of Michael and Mary Van der Loeff. He was educated in Amsterdam and later came to America, settling in San Francisco until after the 1906 earthquake. He came to Spokane about 1907 and established the Van der Loeff Studios, a commercial art firm. He specialized in drawing and painting for the remainder of his life and was well known in Spokane for his talent. On September 16, 1916, he married Ethel (or Eethel) Flewelling Sanderson.

Van der Loeff kept diaries for most of his early life and they are full of the most delightful and fascinating drawings. With the exception of the 1916-1917 diary, they are all written in Dutch. His diaries are located at the MAC.

The artist met Harper Joy in the late 1920s when they were both members of the University Club and working on the silent film *Crown Jewels*. The two were also active in the El Katif Shrine. They remained friends throughout their lives, collaborating on several projects, most notably the Christmas cards the Joys sent every year.

In 1935, when Louis Davenport decided to create the Circus Room in Harper's honor, he enlisted the help of Van der Loeff to create murals covering the entire upper portion of all the walls in the room. This delightful folk art still remains today as a tribute to Harper Joy, a good friend of both Van der Loeff and Davenport. The artist died in 1961 and was cremated.

**A page from one of the Van der Loeff diaries.**

# Fundraising Projects and the Shriners

The years 1939 and 1940 found Harper still enjoying his vacations with the circuses, but also assuming the more important responsibilities of community service. Late in the decade, Whitman College, still struggling to balance its monetary responsibilities, revitalized its Finance Committee and gave the leadership to Harper Joy, along with George Yancey of Spokane and Donald Sherwood of Walla Walla. This trio proceeded to put the college on sound fiscal ground. They have been considered as the most competent money managers in Whitman's history.

In addition to his work for the college, Harper also was named chairman of the March of Dimes in Spokane in 1939; the following year he chaired the Community Chest drive. His abilities as a fundraiser and an organizer were being recognized community-wide.

Another activity important in Harper's life from the time he first came to Spokane was the Shrine. The Shriners' emphasis on having fun, dressing up in costumes and entertaining the public, particularly with circus acts, were all things that would naturally appeal to a man like Harper. He joined the El Katif Temple of Spokane about 1924 and served as ceremonial director from 1936 to 1947. He became a member of the Shrine Directors Association and also was a member of the board of directors of the Spokane unit of the Shriners Hospitals for Children, becoming its chairman in 1959. In October of that year, he was made

**Harper with the El Katif circus wagon.**

an honorary past potentate of El Katif Temple, an honor richly deserved after his 35 years of service.

In 1946-1947 Harper served as president of the National Shrine Directors Association of North America. It truly was an impressive position and great honor. Over the years he enjoyed the association's conventions, parades and entertainment in many cities across America, often accompanied by Dorothy. Everywhere he went, he participated in some way – either by speaking or presenting one of his "acts." Letters he received frequently mention how his contribution made the evening a success.

It has often been said that without men like Harper Joy and the other Shriners, there would not be, in our society today, the really wonderful facilities known as the Shriners Hospitals for Children, one of the finest of these being in Spokane. Harper was actively engaged in the local hospital and in making life better for the young patients there.

## World War II and the Bond Drives

What may have been Harper Joy's greatest contribution to Spokane is one that deserves to be recognized. After the bombing of Pearl Harbor in December 1941, the United States government needed to raise money for the war effort. Spokane's first choice to lead the fund-raising was Roderick A. Lindsay, a banker of tremendous ability and certainly a good choice for the job. (Rod was later to spearhead the effort to make a success of Expo '74.) However, Rod felt his greater service would be to join the armed forces and he enlisted, leaving Spokane without a war bond chairman. In his place they selected Harper Joy, and in 1942 he became the finance chairman for Spokane County. It was a good choice indeed.

**Harper Joy, right, sells the first war bond at an outdoor rally. The purchaser is Edward Edenfield.**

During the war years, Harper's career surpassed anything he had done before. The war bond drives were virtually created for a man of Harper's skills, and he rose to the occasion. He had always felt a certain regret that he had not been able to contribute to World War I, and this opportunity with the war bond drives helped him to compensate for, what he considered, his earlier failure.

# Photos from the War Bond Drives

Jack Dempsey and Harper Joy, 7th War Bond Drive. During the war, Dempsey was appointed to the rank of lieutenant in the United States Coast Guard, and assigned the position of director for physical fitness.

**Hollywood comes to Spokane: Joan Leslie, Adolph Menjou and Walter Pidgeon with Col. William G. Schauffler Jr., commanding officer at Geiger Field in Spokane.**

**Troops from Farragut Naval Station.**

**Pictured left to right: Alan Ladd, unknown gentleman, George Ingraham Jr., Bruce Cabot and Harper Joy.**

**Women's Army Corps (WACs).**

Reviewing stand. Spokane Mayor F. G. Sutherlin on the far left.

Women's Army Corps, marching past the Davenport Hotel.

**Harper and his army of volunteers.**

**Army Corps of Engineers.**

**North Central High School marching band.**

**Military equipment on parade.**

Second bond drive, September 1943
Harper Joy presiding.

Fifth bond drive,
war bond poster.

Harper's enthusiasm and expertise in helping the war effort could hardly diminish what was going on in his own home. Midway through the war, a grand surprise was presented to Harper and Dorothy. Their fourth child and third son, Edward Mendenhall Joy, was born on December 1, 1943. He proved to be a

Edward "Eddie"
Mendenhall Joy
born December 1, 1943
"King Edward the IV"

wonderful little brother to the other Joy children and, in later years, a comfort and help to both his father and mother.

By now the United States was fully engaged in the war effort, and patriotism was at an all time high. No one could have been better equipped than Harper Joy to create a successful atmosphere for giving, and his name became synonymous with savings bonds. Through his efforts thousands of volunteers became an integrated force, helping Spokane County meet and surpass every bond quota during the war years. During this period, he had the help of numerous Spokane businessmen, most notably his boss and friend, Joel Ferris, as well as Harry Goetz, John T. Little, George Ingraham Jr., and H. L. Barrett, and numerous others. Harper's job was to coordinate the efforts of all involved, no small task.

Harper approached the bond drives from the perspective of entertainment – when people were entertained, they were inspired to contribute. It was a wonderful two-way street. The U.S. government had a volunteer bureau consisting of popular film, sports and radio stars who were willing to appear at fund raisers for the war effort, and Harper was just the right man to enlist their help. Every bond drive featured celebrities, who appeared in downtown Spokane to urge the purchase of war bonds. The armed forces cooperated by seeing that bands and marching units were available for the parades, and there were local musicians and heroes to complement the rest. Harper's son Benjamin remembered the stands set up on Riverside and the big parades. Newberry's store at the corner had a display of the armaments that would be purchased with war bond money. Ben never forgot the excitement of it all.

There were eight bond drives in all, but the third was the one Harper enjoyed the most. The parade featured a corps of Army Engineers, a WAC color guard of the flags of the 33 allied nations, a unit from Farragut Naval Station, and proudly for Spokane, the band from North Central High School. As Harper was later to say: "The parade was the greatest ever seen in Spokane and took nearly one hour to pass a given point." It produced almost five million dollars more than the quota expected. The drives to follow proved to be even greater, and the financial results of all of them are astounding.

The summary of the Spokane County War Loans tells the story in terms that are easily understood. The first column indicates Spokane County's quota; the second records the total sales:

| | | |
|---|---|---|
| 1st War Loan | - - - | $ 6,500,000 |
| 2nd " " | $ 8,402,620 | 13,024,454 |
| 3rd " " | 18,000,000 | 22,832,084 |
| 4th " " | 17,500,000 | 22,407,252 |
| 5th " " | 22,000,000 | 30,478,550 |
| 6th " " | 17,400,000 | 30,338,735 |
| 7th " " | 18,540,000 | 27,203,746 |
| 8th " " | 12,980,000 | 28,650,584 |
| | $ 114,822,620 | $ 181,435,405 |

Following the conclusion of the final Victory Loan, William C. H. Lewis, the executive manager of the War Finance Committee, Washington State Treasury Department, announced on June 17, 1946 to all county chairmen that the total sales in Spokane County amounted to $243,321,501, about nine percent of the state total. This was a tribute not only to Harper Joy and the men who had assisted him, but also to the city of Spokane and to Spokane County, where citizens and private businesses were amazingly generous during the war years to produce these results.

In 1946 the Washington State Treasury Department, Office of State Administrator, awarded silver medals to the following Spokane citizens for their contributions to the war bond drives:

| | |
|---|---|
| Harper Joy | Ross McElroy |
| Joel E. Ferris | Nave Lien |
| Harry Goetz | E. W. Baker |
| Raymond Kelly | Jos. M. Tewinkel |
| John T. Little | George Ingraham Jr. |
| Chauncey Adams | Will H. Murgittroyd |
| Frank Tool | Wallace Brazeal |
| Paul Schiffner | Roderick Lindsay |
| E. D. Raddatz | Geo. O. Hackett |
| Justin McWilliams | Virginia Rogers |
| Joseph Cornelius | Leonard Musser |
| Ralph Austin | Gordon Hockaday |

Harper received numerous letters applauding his efforts on behalf of the war effort. Spokane's Commissioner of Public Safety William Payne expressed his feelings this way: "When working with men of your caliber, it is very easy to accomplish any task. I consider it an honor, as well as a privilege, to assist you in anything at all, so please feel free to call on me at any time."

During the war years Harper was privileged to meet a number of important and interesting people. One of them was Ralph Edwards, the radio announcer and emcee who had been part of the *Truth or Consequences* radio show for several years. The two met in a show held at Geiger Field on April 28, 1943. Edwards was impressed with this Spokane man, who was a businessman and a clown, and was to remember him a few years later when he began a new radio series called *This Is Your Life*.

# The Last Act:
# THE POST WAR YEARS

As the war finally drew to a close, life became a little less frantic for the Joy family. Dorothy and the children, including two-year-old Ed, enjoyed having Harper around more often. During the war Harper had become a trustee of Whitman College. He and the family had frequently visited Walla Walla in the previous years to see his mother. In addition, these trips gave him the opportunity to attend to his business affairs at Whitman College.

On March 8, 1946, Annie Joy died in Walla Walla at age 86. She had been a widow for 19 years, as her husband Henry had died March 9, 1927. Her obituary stated that she was survived by sons Harper Joy of Spokane, and Harry H.

**Annie Joy, shortly before her death in 1946.**

Joy of Portland, and daughter Irene MacIntosh of San Francisco. In the fall of that year, Nancy Joy was ready for college and enrolled at Whitman. She would have preferred to attend an art school, as she was artistically inclined like her mother and grandmother, but Harper was so dedicated to his alma mater that he felt Whitman was the necessary choice. This was probably an unfair position to take, but Harper Joy was sometimes a man of very inflexible opinions and his high regard for Whitman College was one of them.

Harper was always on the lookout for ways to promote his alma mater. Near the close of the war Harper met a young veteran, newly discharged, who came to Spokane looking for a job. His name was Pete Reid. Harper recognized him as a person who needed a goal and deserved help. His assistance in enabling Pete to enroll at Whitman was important both to the young man and to the school. Pete Reid not only graduated in 1949 but has remained at the college ever since. He has served in many capacities, but at present is a special assistant to the president. He credits Harper Joy for his career.

**The Joy family in their new library, 1949. Standing: Ben, Nancy and Jim; Seated: Dorothy, Ed and Harper. Notice the circus wagon on the top shelf at the right.**

The Joy children were growing up fast, although young Eddie still had a way to go. Harper and Dorothy had the pleasure of remodeling their home, turning the sunroom into a paneled library. It was a fine addition, as there was now a place to stash their books and other collectibles. One of the latter was a circus wagon, which held a place of honor on the top shelf.

## Ralph Edwards and *This Is Your Life*

On January 4, 1949, Harper flew to Los Angeles at the request of Ralph Edwards, for what he thought would be an interview-type radio show, where Ralph would get him to talk about his circus experiences. It was his surprise to find himself the guest of honor on *This Is Your Life*. Edwards, already a veteran NBC radio announcer, had started the show on April 27, 1946, as a vehicle to publicize and honor ordinary people who did extraordinary things. The show was immensely popular and boasted a large share of the radio audience. In the half-hour episodes, the honoree was presented with the story of his life, including surprise visits from family, friends and associates. Harper Joy was the tenth person to be so honored. The guests on Harper's show included his YMCA friend F. D. Applegate; his

**Ralph Edwards presents his *This Is Your Life* guest with a watercolor painting of Harper as a clown.**

**The circus wagon, one of the family's favorite mementos of Harper, now holds a place of prominence at the Liberty Lake cottage.** *(Bamonte photo)*

sister Irene; Elsie Bowen, the woman who had urged Harper to go to college; several circus friends including Leonard Gross, Charlie Post and a female acrobat whose husband had received help from Harper many years before. Also a surprise was Harper's wonderful long-time secretary from Ferris & Hardgrove, Margaret Stickney. Dorothy, of course, was there and charmed the audience. The highlight of the show was the performance of the "Harper Joy Triumphal March," played in true circus-orchestra style and conducted by its composer, Charlie Post.

Ralph Edwards had some further surprises for Harper. He presented him with a watercolor picture of Harper as a clown, which now hangs in the lobby of the Harper Joy Theatre at Whitman College. In addition, August 31st would be "Harper Joy Day" at circuses throughout the United States to celebrate his birthday.

Listening to a tape of the program is reminiscent of the nostalgic time when radio was the foremost entertainment medium of the day. Harper's surprise and pleasure in the experience are evident. The recording is poor in places, with spots when the listener can't tell what's going on. Thanks to the laughter of the audience, however, one can visualize that Harper was perhaps doing a soft-shoe routine or some other bit of schtick at the time.

The half-hour radio show was only the beginning of what was to come for Harper Joy. Fortunately, he kept all the letters and wires that he received afterwards and, in true Harper Joy style, had them bound into a two-inch thick book. To Harper, it was "one of the greatest experiences" of his life. Following his appearance on the show, he received at least 30 telegrams and more than 145 letters from old friends and new and, according to Harper, "a virtual blizzard of correspondence." Harper respected Ralph Edwards and they remained friends. Later, in his usual wise and introspective way, Harper wrote to Edwards: "I realize now, more than ever, that the human interest in the program was not so much Harper Joy as it was the adaptation by your listeners of experiences in my life to those in theirs."

The letters came from every corner of the United States and from circus, investment and railroad people, as well as old acquaintances from Walla Walla and Spokane. Without exception, they were all enthusiastic and in agreement that Harper and Dorothy were wonderful radio personalities. Some were especially interesting – following is just a sampling:

1) A letter from an adoptive mother, asking his advice about telling their six-year-old daughter that she was adopted. Harper's reply: "By all means do that, for I know from my own experience that some smart alec ... will throw it up to the child." He also commended her for adopting a little helpless child ... "their lives would be enriched by it."

2) A letter from a Navy nurse at Farragut Naval Base in Idaho, who had met Harper at the Press Club in Spokane, when he gave her and her friend a complimentary pass to use at the club during their stint at the naval base. She had never forgotten his kindness.

3) A few people asked for money (for worthwhile causes, of course!) and a Massachusetts man was looking for a job in a new location.

4) An old friend who was so proud he felt "a little chesty" about their friendship.

5) The secretary with a New York investment firm who added her P.S.: "I envy your secretary – the investment bankers here are such inveterate golfers."

6) A friend from Chicago who had gone to school with Jack Benny and "now knew two radio stars."

7) The *Sedalia Democrat* (Harper's place of birth) asking for a bio and picture of their favorite son, which they wanted to publish (and did).

8) A letter to Dorothy from an 80-year-old man who had known her father, Mark Mendenhall. He and Mark met in Ohio in 1891 and became very good friends, later renewing their friendship in Spokane. He enclosed a picture of Mark and added that he was glad that Dorothy also had such a wonderful husband.

9) A letter from Margaret Broughel, the widow of the man who had hired him when he came back to Walla Walla from vaudeville. Harper's reply to her: "When I told him I wanted to go to Whitman, he said 'I'm going to work out a job here so you can do both.'" It meant the world to Harper.

10) Certainly the most amazing of all was a letter from Pearl Fitch Reiber of Montserrrat, Missouri, and it wasn't received until March 30th, so it was one of the later letters. Pearl had seen the article in the *Sedalia Democrat* and informed Harper that she was a personal friend of his birth mother, Anna Harper, and her parents; had met his father, John Lounsbury, as well; and had known Harper as a young baby. The news was of paramount importance to Harper. He corresponded with Mrs. Reiber, learning things he had never known about his birth parents and his grandparents. He soon met Mrs. Reiber on a trip to Missouri and was able to erect a tombstone on the grave of his grandfather Josiah Harper and donate money to the cemetery where he was buried. None of this would ever have happened had he not appeared on the Ralph Edwards show. Harper felt that, indeed, "Life deals some strange chapters."

The Ralph Edwards show was not Harper's last venture into radio. In August there was a series from Spokane called *Portrait of a City*, and Harper appeared on one segment of the series. By an odd coincidence, a friend in Buffalo, New York, heard the show and wrote to Harper that he had "outperformed Bing Crosby and did a far better job of selling Spokane." I don't doubt it for a minute!

## The Later Years

If you think that things were winding down for Harper Joy, you would be wrong. He was still actively involved with Whitman College and, on the home front, Ferris & Hardgrove had moved ahead to become the Pacific Northwest Company. In 1953 the firm celebrated its 40th anniversary with a gala event at the Davenport Hotel. In addition, Harper also found time to participate in the newly formed Civic Theatre and received a favorable review for his performance in *Life With Father*. Other activities that kept things stirring for Harper were groups such as the Royal Court of Jesters and the Rotary Club. Not surprisingly, he was included in the 1954 issue of *Who's Who In America*. With him that year were other Whitman dignitaries: William O. Douglas, Ralph J. Cordiner and Stephen B. L. Penrose Jr.

Another unexpected phase of the Joys' life began when, in 1957, daughter Nancy married Pierre Salinger, who became John F. Kennedy's press secretary. Although Harper was a staunch Republican, he enjoyed getting to know his new son-in-law and had the pleasure of meeting John Kennedy when the presidential candidate was in Spokane during the campaign. In August of 1961, during the Salingers' visit to Spokane, Harper arranged a luncheon for Pierre, attended by many of Spokane's most influential people, including many from the television stations and the *Spokesman-Review*.

By this time, the Joy family had returned to just three – Harper, Dorothy and Ed. The Christmas card of 1960 reflects the smaller family, and the picture on the card is choice–the three of them eating under an umbrella in the rain. One of the recipients, Shriner pal Lou Chackes, couldn't resist submitting his poetic opinion:

> *Your Holiday Card brought many thoughts to mind*
>   *Most of 'em Merry – but there's also the other kind.*
> *F'rinstance – the trio's laughing – all seem to be glad.*
>   *Eddie, the under-cover man – Dar, too – but how about Dad?*
> *I can overlook many things, but am easily provoked*
>   *When others hog the shelter – while Harp gets soaked.*
> *Bareheaded, Eddie laughs – he suffers no pain*
>   *While Dad – oh joy – is singing out in the rain.*
> *Jest the same – May Heaven's choicest blessings shower on You*
>   *Is the fervent prayer of your pal*
>                                         *Merrily! Lou*

Life for Harper and Dorothy was also beginning to blossom. They began to travel in earnest and took several lengthy trips to Central America, Mexico and Europe. Eventually they traveled around the world. Most of these were not pre-planned "tours" but were rather freelance sightseeing journeys, going from place to place as the spirit moved them. It was a wonderful way to travel, and Dorothy found a new and exciting avocation – photography. She also expanded her wonderful collection of Madonna figurines from all over the world. It was not "just a collection." When she returned home, she used her imagination and artistic skills to present these multi-national creations in interesting and beautiful ways. Her efforts were rewarded with an exceptionally well-written article in the *Sunday Magazine* of the *Spokesman-Review* on December 15, 1968.

From the Joy Christmas card, 1960. Harper, Dorothy and Ed enjoying a picnic in the rain.

Pierre Salinger and Harper Joy, August 1961.

## Senator Kennedy in Spokane

The caption below this photo reads: "Harper Joy of Spokane (left) chats with Senator John F. Kennedy (D. Mass.) yesterday during the presidential hopeful's visit here. Joy's son-in-law, Pierre Salinger, is Senator Kennedy's press secretary. The senator's principal address here was before a Jefferson-Jackson day crowd at the Davenport Hotel." *(Spokesman-Review Februray 12, 1960)*

Although Harper was an avowed Republican, he was favorably impressed with John Kennedy, and contributed to his campaign fund. However, according to Harper's son Ed when it came time to vote, Harper admitted he had voted for Richard Nixon.

# THE EARLY SPOKANE THEATRE SCENE

Harper Joy never lost his interest in the theatrical side of life. As a man who loved performing, he was involved in amateur groups from his earliest days in Spokane. One of the first of these was the Drama Group, whose beginnings are obscure, but eventually, in 1926, found their first home in the Brunot Apartments.

A promotional picture for the Civic Theatre production of *Life With Father*. John H. Happy, left, is seen as Dr. Somers, and next to him is Harper, playing the Reverend Dr. Lloyd. The actress playing the maid has not been identified.

The Brunot Apartments were created from the original Brunot School, an Episcopalian school for girls founded by Bishop Lemuel H. Wells in the late 1890s. It was named for its endower, Felix Brunot of Pittsburgh, Pennsylvania. The school was located at the corner of Pacific and Hemlock, behind Patsy Clark's mansion, and was successful and highly respected for many years. However, by the time World War I was in progress, the school began to face financial problems, due in large part to the vast improvements going on with the local public high schools. In 1917 the school closed and the building was converted to apartments.

In 1926 the Drama Group took over a portion of the apartment building and converted it to a theatre, using the name of the "Alley Playhouse," probably because it was located at the rear of the building on the alley between their building and the Clark mansion. Their first performance was *The Torch Bearers* on February 16, 1926, which they performed at the Masonic Temple Auditorium, as the stage at Brunot was not yet ready.

By 1928 this group was known as the Spokane Little Theatre and was located at 1019 First Avenue. Harper Joy was the business manager for this little theatre for eight years, occasionally performing on the stage.

In 1947 the Little Theatre became the Spokane Civic Theatre, whose success over the ensuing years is well documented. Their first presentation, which ran from February to April 1947, was *State of the Union*, starring

Dorothy Darby Smith. In those days the stage performances were presented at the State Theatre, which usually showed movies, so that the theatricals had to make do with the evenings in between. Harper had the pleasure of performing in one of the State Theatre showings, *Life With Father* by Howard Lindsay and Russell Crouse and directed by Dorothy Darby Smith. Harper played the part of the Reverend Dr. Lloyd, and old friend John Happy portrayed Dr. Somers.

Harper was well acquainted with Dorothy Darby Smith, who is generally recognized as the "Grande Dame of Spokane Theatre." For many years, Dorothy's mother, Ethel Welliver, worked for the Pacific Northwest Co. (formerly Ferris & Hardgrove) and was well known to Harper in business affairs. John Happy was another long-time acquaintance of Harper's, as they had been neighbors on Twenty-first Avenue.

By 1957 the Civic Theatre was performing at a location on Riverside, and finally in 1967 was gratified to have its own building on North 1020 Howard, where it has been located ever since. Harper and Dorothy Joy were members of the Spokane Civic Theatre for many years and supported its remarkable growth with pleasure.

**Above is a Rotary Club entertainment in 1930. Harper is kneeling center front The picture was taken along the east wall of the Elizabethan Room at the Davenport Hotel, showing the secret door to Louis Davenport's office on the mezzanine (the hinge is visible to the left of the sconce light fixture).**

"Get together" at Harper's office in Spokane about 1953. Left to right: George Yancey of Murphey-Favre in Spokane; Dr. David Gaiser of Spokane whose wife, Mary Jewett Gaiser, was a Whitman trustee; Supreme Court Justice William O. Douglas; and Harper Joy.

## Honors from Whitman College

On June 13, 1948, Harper was honored with a Doctor of Laws degree by Whitman College, together with classmate and Phi Delt brother Ralph Cordiner. It was a proud moment. Needless to say, he received a grand assortment of letters concerning this achievement. His old friend, Shriner Lou Chackes, said it best: "Doctor sorta sounds natural – for you have always been a refreshing tonic and master of calm and wise decision. More power to you!"

Through all of his years in Spokane, he had been involved in some way with this Walla Walla college, and there is no doubt that his contributions were exceptional and appreciated. He wasn't alone in this. It speaks volumes for the impact this college had on his life and on those of the other prominent members of his class. These men were all fortunate to be able to support the school financially, but they also gave of their time and energy, perhaps even more important to the ultimate success of the institution. The finance committee was shrewd in its investments and tried always to find those that were best suited to Whitman. There were personal rewards for this, but they were not financial. Cordiner Hall

The Pacific Northwest Company (formerly Ferris & Hardgrove) celebrated its 40th anniversary with a dinner party at the Davenport Hotel, honoring its executive vice president, Harper Joy. Note the many circus pictures and posters on the wall, some of which were given to the Circus Fans of America and others still to be found at the Liberty Lake cottage. Back row: Sam Whittemore, Earl Dusenbery, Maj. Bill Roberts, two unidentified women, Harper Joy, Ethel Welliver, an unidentified man. Front row: George Ingraham, Estelle Whittemore, Stanley Minor, unidentified woman, Al Peterson, unidentified woman, Laura Morrison.

bears the name of Ralph Cordiner, one of the trustees, and Sherwood Center, of course, was named for another illustrious Whitman alumnus, Donald Sherwood. But many of the school's officials considered Harper Joy to be one of the most capable of the trustees – "Energetic, positive, and personable."

By 1967, Harper felt, because of his age, it was time to resign from the Whitman Board of Trustees, and the college honored his outstanding service by naming Whitman's theatre building the "Harper Joy Theatre." Nothing could have been a greater honor or thrill for Harper and his family. It was a wonderful tribute to this man who cared so much about both the college and the theatre.

**Back row: Joel Ferris, Dorothy Joy, Harold Cameron, Edith Smith, Helene Ingraham, Earl Morrison, and Margaret Stickney (Harper's secretary). Front row: unidentified woman, Mrs. Al Peterson, Colonel Ralph Phelps, three unidentified women. The china on the tables in this and the picture on the preceding page is from the Davenports' personal service, selected by Mrs. Davenport. It is Castleton china, the same company that provided the china at the White House. The pattern is "Laurel," and pieces of this service are on display at the hotel today. The room was probably a "sample room," similar to the Circus Room.**

The Harper Joy Theatre was dedicated in June of 1967, and the plaque at the entrance reads:

"IN HONOR OF
HIS LONG AND ENDURING
SERVICE AND DEVOTION TO THE
COLLEGE AND THEATRE AS A
STUDENT, TRUSTEE, BENEFACTOR
AND WARM FRIEND."

Also in the lobby of the theatre are pictures of Harper: the one he received from Ralph Edwards on *This Is Your Life* and the other a portrait of him taken shortly before the dedication ceremony.

In the printed program published for the ceremony, the following items are listed:

| | |
|---|---|
| Introduction | Dr. Louis Barnes Perry, President of the College |
| Dedication | Donald Sherwood, President of the Board of Trustees |
| Presentation | Rodney Wilson Alexander, Director of the Theatre. |
| Response | Harper Joy, B.S., LL.D. |
| Honored Guest | Dorothy Mendenhall Joy |

For Dorothy and Harper, it was the culmination of his years as an entertainer.

On May 4, 1985, there was a rededication ceremony of the theatre, which had been renovated thanks to the money raised by friend and Phi Delta Theta brother Don Sherwood. By this time Harper was gone, but Dorothy attended, and she later sent the following letter to the college:

> Harper Joy's family of Nancy, Jim, Benny, Ed and I, as well as my sister and brother, are delighted with the enlarged and restored Harper Joy Theatre. Harper would love it–he reveled in having a theatre named for him. ... Whitman enriched Harper's life enormously, opening windows and avenues to him. He loved Whitman with all his heart and showed his devotion by his untiring efforts in Whitman's behalf.
>
> We greatly appreciate Whitman's decision to do this, and want to extend our deep thanks to all the alumni who have contributed to make it possible, among them my cousin Mary Helen McCrea, '20, who had the fountain installed.

Many thanks,
Dorothy Mendenhall Joy, '26

**Harper Joy Theatre, Whitman College.** *(Doris Woodward photo)*

**Harper Joy's resignation from the Whitman Board of Trustees, July 1, 1967. Don Sherwood on the left, and Louis B. Perry, Whitman president, on the right.**

# THE JOY CHILDREN
## Nancy Brook Joy

Nancy was born in Spokane on April 2, 1928, a beautiful baby and the first to occupy the nursery at 825 West Twenty-first Avenue. She graduated from Lewis & Clark High School and attended Whitman College, where she was a member of Delta Delta Delta sorority (more commonly known as "Tri Delt"), as was her mother before her. Upon graduation, Nancy went to California to work. After several years she met and married a man who was becoming important in American politics. His name was Pierre Salinger. At the time she met him, he was an editor in California for *Collier's* magazine.

Nancy and Pierre were married on June 28, 1957, after which he spent two years as an investigator for Robert Kennedy on a Senate Select Committee investigating labor-union racketeering, in particular the activities of Dave Beck. Salinger's efforts impressed Bobby, who convinced his brother Senator John Kennedy to use Salinger to assist in the coming election campaign. Salinger's organizing abilities were outstanding. Following the election he remained with the Kennedy administration, serving as the White House press secretary.

**Nancy Brook Joy,
about 1938.**

Because of the association with the Kennedy administration, Nancy's marriage to Salinger was in many ways her "claim to fame." But actually, Nancy's recollection of those years tells a different story. In a *Spokesman-Review* interview on November 20, 1983, she admitted that she found herself askew with "Camelot" and was from the start "a little uncomfortable with the Kennedy mystique and elegance."

It was typical of her day, in politics and in big business, that the "little woman" was simply an adjunct to her husband. It was a part of the American culture that was soon to be on its way out. Nancy found herself resenting it. She had grown up as "Harper Joy's daughter" and was now "Pierre Salinger's wife." Nancy needed to be a person in her own right.

There is no doubt there were times when she enjoyed herself immensely and was the "belle of the ball." "It was glittering ... how many people can say they have danced at the White House? There I was just a little girl from Spokane, overwhelmed by all of those important people." After the assassination of John Kennedy, Nancy found that Lyndon and Lady Bird Johnson were easier to

**Nancy Joy, freshman at Whitman College, 1950.**

know than the Kennedys. She and Pierre were invited to the presidential quarters on the third floor of the White House, a part of the building they had never before seen. She obviously appreciated this friendly gesture on the part of the Johnsons. Soon after, in 1964, Salinger returned to California to run for the U.S. Senate, and Harper, Dorothy and Ed joined him on a whistle-stop campaign. Nancy campaigned vigorously for her husband, but Pierre lost the election to movie star George Murphy. By 1965, the marriage between Nancy and Pierre was over.

Nancy remained in the area around Washington, D.C., and since she wished to pursue an artistic career, she started "The Joy of Pottery" school in Columbia, Maryland. She designed and produced pottery for sale and exhibition, winning several awards. She also taught pottery classes. Her artistic abilities are certainly a legacy from those of her mother and her grand-mother. In 1967 she married John Botzum. Their son, Keys Dylan Botzum, was born in 1968. Nancy has since divorced John and still resides in Columbia, where she continues teaching her pottery classes. For many years John Botzum was the president of Nautilus Press, a small company that published newsletters concerning the oceans and their health. John died in 2003.

**Nancy Joy today, with her son, Keys Botzum.** *(Photo courtesy of Keys Botzum)*

Keys is currently a senior technical staff member with IBM in Maryland and also lives in Columbia. He and Nancy come west each summer to spend a few weeks at the Liberty Lake cottage, where Nancy still enjoys a long swim almost every day.

Pierre Salinger's campaign for the U.S. Senate in California. Left to right: Marc Salinger, Harper Joy, Dan Blocker (who played Hoss Cartwright on the TV show *Bonanza*), Pierre Salinger, unidentified woman, Dorothy Joy and Ed Joy.

## James Harper Joy II

James Harper Joy II was born in Spokane on March 8, 1931. After spending his freshman year at Hill Military Academy in Portland, he attended Lewis & Clark High School and graduated in 1949. During the Korean War, he served in the United States Navy, Amphibious Forces Pacific. He entered Whitman College in 1954, where like his father he was a member of Phi Delta Theta. In 1957 he graduated with a BA in English and political science. This was not to be the end of his education, however, as he went on to graduate studies at the University of Vienna, Oxford University and the American School of Classical Studies at Athens. By 1965 he received an MA in government from the School of Public Affairs at the American University, Washington, D.C.

**Jimmy Joy, about 1941.**

James was in government service from 1958 to 1982, initially as a research assistant to Robert F. Kennedy and the U.S. Senate Select Committee on La-

**James Joy, Whitman College, 1956.**

bor Rackets. Later he was a campaign assistant to Senator John F. Kennedy, an information science specialist with the National Aeronautics and Space Administration, and an associate director of the Information Science Program, National Science Foundation. He was an instructor in humanities, teaching a "Great Books" course at Howard University in Washington, D.C., from 1970 to 1977.

After retiring from federal service, he became associated in Arlington, Virginia, with the Central Library and the public schools. In 1988 he entered George Mason University for a doctoral program in history and taught American History and European Civilization as an adjunct professor of history at Northern Virginia Community College in Woodbridge. He was awarded a doctorate in history in 2001; a revised version of his dissertation, published in Ireland in 2002 by the University College Dublin Press, was entitled *Victory and Woe*: *The West Limerick Brigade in the War of Independence*, a "Classic of Irish History."

His interest in Ireland was spurred by his marriage on May 20, 1961, to Bridget "Bridie" Christina Harnett of Dublin, whom he met when he was working for

**James and Bridie Joy in the library of their home, 1990.**

John Kennedy and she was secretary to the Irish Ambassador in Washington. They have continued to live in Arlington, Virginia, and have three children who were raised there: Eileen Aroon Joy, who is a professor of English at the University of Southern Illinois at Edwardsville; Deirdre Alana Joy, a program officer in molecular biology at the National Institute of Health; and James Harper Joy III of Denver, Colorado, a restoration contractor, whose interests center on historic preservation. One of his recent projects was the restoration of the county courthouse in Telluride, Colorado.

James and Bridie have often returned to the Spokane area to spend a few weeks at Liberty Lake and to renew old acquaintances in Spokane. He is retired now, but continues to have many interests, among them traveling and writing poetry. He is a man of class and intelligence, which speaks volumes for his upbringing as a son of Harper and Dorothy Joy.

"BROTHER ALUMNUS HAS A SON"

And in Washington Beta and many other chapters—one learns as he reads the under-
graduate letters in this issue—he's welcomed joyfully into the great brotherhood of
Phi Delta Theta. This picture was selected for our cover as fittingly representative of
scenes which took place in Phi houses throughout the realm of the Fraternity in recent
weeks, as Phi fathers proudly extended the grip to their sons as Brothers in the Bond.
At Whitman former class- and chapter-mates Harry Jesseph (left) and Harper Joy, '22,
congratulate their newly initiated sons, Jerry and Harper, Jr.

★ ★ ★ THE ★ ★ ★

SCROLL

MARCH
•
1951

OF PHI DELTA THETA

VOLUME LXXV        NUMBER 4

Cover of the Phi Delta Theta *Scroll*, March 1951. Father and son, James and
Harper Joy are on the right, after Jim's initiation into the fraternity.

# Benjamin Lounsbury Joy

Ben was born in Spokane on March 18, 1932 and attended Wilson Elementary School and Lewis & Clark High School like his sister Nancy and brother Jim. One of his high school years he spent at Hill Military Academy in Portland. Ben loved music, and during grade and high school always played either the trumpet or the trombone in band and musical events. Unlike his sister and brothers, he was not interested in going to college. After graduating from high school, Ben went to California, where he attended the Westlake School of Music in Hollywood for three years. He joined a quintet that traveled widely, performing at Lake Tahoe, Las Vegas, Reno, Toronto, and through the Midwest. They played dance music at supper clubs. Ben always said their leader had a voice "like Perry Como."

Benny Joy, about 1942.

Poster featuring Benny Joy and his Star Dusters, Liberty Lake.

In 1955 Ben married Carma Duval, and the couple had two daughters, Cathleen and Dorothy, but the marriage didn't last. He retained custody of the children, however, and found himself often touring around the country with two little girls in tow, sometimes hiring a nanny to travel with them. Eventually he organized his own group, which was called "Benny Joy and the Three Joys." They were a successful combo, and toured across the United States as far as Florida. When they finally made the rounds to Alaska, Ben found the country so much to his liking that he chose to remain there.

Ben married again, on November 6, 1961, in Anchorage, Alaska. His second wife was Jacqueline "Jackie" Hamilton, a girl from Montana. The couple enjoyed their life in the north, where they raised and showed Great Danes. The couple also spent much of their spare time fishing and hunting. For many years Ben worked for the State of Alaska in the Wage and Hour Division of the Department of Labor, keeping music as an avocation. Sadly, his wife died on February 19, 2006. His daughters still live in the area, and gave Ben four grandsons, one granddaughter and one great-grandson and provided him with a very satisfying family life.

**Jackie and Ben with daughters Cathleen and Dorothy, at a family reunion at Liberty Lake, 1963.**

Ben was a natural entertainer and a musician. He also always enjoyed speaking and performing in front of crowds of people, abilities he certainly inherited from his father. Harper and Dorothy visited him in Alaska in the years when they were still traveling. Ben was a confirmed Alaskan and, due to ill health in later years, he didn't get back to Washington State very often.

Benjamin Lounsbury Joy died on April 18, 2007, and his sister and brothers traveled to Alaska for the services and to be with Ben's daughters and their families. Ben was pleased to know that this story about his father was being written, and the author is glad she had the opportunity to be in touch with him before his death.

## Edward Mendenhall Joy

Edward Mendenhall Joy was born in Spokane on December 1, 1943, the youngest by many years of the Joy children. When Harper wrote about his children in later years, he remarked that Eddie had "come on a late train." He was named after Harper's brother Eddie, who had died in the fire in Walla Walla. His middle name, of course, was his mother's maiden name. After graduating from Lewis & Clark High School in 1962, he attended Whitman College from 1962

**A group of Spokane children being entertained by clown Emmett Kelly Sr., as he provides a treat to young Ed Joy. Inset; Ed Joy, age 10.**

to 1966, joined Phi Delta Theta, like his father and brother, and graduated with a BA in political science.

Looking toward a career in law, he enrolled in the Gonzaga University Law School, eventually reaching this goal, but not for many years. Following a year at Gonzaga, he enrolled at Whitworth College in education, obtaining a secondary teaching certificate. This led to a teaching job at Oakville High School in Grays Harbor County, where he taught a variety of courses, including civics, history and (his favorite) auto mechanics.

At Oakville Ed met his future wife, Linda Sue Grimes, and his life took some surprising turns. Linda was from Pennsylvania, a history major, graduating from Muskingum College in New Concord, Ohio, in 1968. She was assigned to the Chehalis Indian Reservation representing VISTA (Volunteers in Service to America). Ed and Linda fell in love, and even though Ed enjoyed teaching at Oakville, when Linda was through with her assignment with VISTA, they went to Pennsylvania, where Ed roomed with Linda's family and found a teaching job in Norwalk, Ohio, for the 1969-70 school year, teaching history and civics. The couple was married December 22, 1969. Ed finished the school year in Norwalk, and Linda obtained a teaching certificate from Heidelberg College. That summer they moved to Spokane, where they lived on Moran Prairie. It was a lot of moving around for a young man and his wife and was vaguely reminiscent of Harper Joy's extensive wanderlust in his early years.

**The Ed Joy family. Back row: Dan Karalus, Susan Joy Karalus, Linda and Ed. Front row: Melissa, Natalie and Eddie.**

Ed returned to his first interest–law–and spent the next three years at Gonzaga. He passed the Washington State Bar Exam in 1973 and was admitted to practice the fall of that year, joining the law firm of Wolff and Eberle for 1974 and 1975. Somehow the young couple was not completely satisfied with this life and took the daring step of purchasing a 300-acre farm south of Coeur d'Alene, Idaho. Although Ed's intent was to start a small-town law practice somewhere in the area, this never happened, and farming has been his vocation ever since.

Ed and Linda have four children, all a source of pride to their parents:

1. Susan Elizabeth graduated from Gustavus Adolphus College in Saint Peter, Minnesota, majoring in geology, and earned an MA in geology from the University of Montana. She and husband Dan Karalus, also a graduate of Gustavus Adolphus, live in Boise, Idaho. Dan earned his MA in environmental history at the University of Idaho. On September 20, 2007, Susan and Dan became the parents of their first son, Harper Daniel Karalus.

2. Natalie Irene graduated from Reed College in Portland, spent a year as an Americorps volunteer (similar to her mother's VISTA experience) and is pursuing a PhD in American history at UCLA.

3. Edward Mendenhall II graduated from Whitman College, majoring in mathematics, and is now an auto mechanic in Missoula.

4. Melissa Brook graduated from Pacific Lutheran University in Tacoma, majoring in Spanish, and is employed at the Boise City Library.

For many years Ed has been on the board of the Kootenai County (Idaho) Public Library, and both he and Linda enjoy a variety of activities. Ed continues a lifelong interest in antique automobiles from the '20s and '30s. Because he was so many years younger than the other Joy children and the only one who stayed in the Spokane area, Ed was really his parents' sustainer as they grew older, especially of his mother after Harper died. He is also the keeper of all the family memorabilia and the archivist of the Joy and Mendenhall legacy.

## The Children's Memories

Each of the children has unique memories from childhood. All are in accord that life was not always easy. They all acknowledge that their father was away from home a great deal and agree that their mother often had to cope with problems by herself. Fortunately she had the network of her Mendenhall family for support.

**Nancy and Ed at the Spokane airport before the family reunion at Liberty Lake, 1963.**

The Joy family at the family reunion at Liberty Lake. Back row: Dorothy, Harper and Nancy. Front row: Ed, Ben and Jim.

Harper had a quick temper, and would blow up on occasion, although he was equally quick to forgive. He was not a perfectionist, but he was very organized, a trait he needed for the life he lived. Dorothy, on the other hand, was what the children describe as "laid back." Organization was not her forte. The two personalities sometimes were in conflict, but it was an example of the old adage, "opposites attract." All the children have been proud of their heritage and remember their days at 825 West Twenty-first with fondness.

# The Curtain Comes Down

Harper Joy died on May 22, 1972, at the age of 77. He had been in failing health for some time and had recently been injured in a fall. His obituaries in the Spokane newspapers, the *Walla Walla Union Bulletin* and *The Scroll* of Phi Delta Theta were full of accounts of his accomplishments.

Additional interests of Harper are mentioned in his obituaries. To name the most significant: he was a director of Columbia Electric Company, a past director of the Sunshine Mining Company, a member of the Board of Governors and vice president of the National Association of Securities Dealers, and on the Board of Fairmount Memorial Park for many years. He also belonged to the City Club, Press Club and University Club.

Harper's funeral, with the Rose Croix Scottish Rite of Freemasonry participating, was held at Westminster Congregational Church, at the corner of Fourth Avenue and Washington. His pallbearers were Horton Herman, Earl Dusenbery, George Kellogg, William C. Roberts, Harold Sampson and Harry Wiedeman. The honorary pallbearers included many of Spokane and Walla Walla's most familiar names: Jack Dishman, R. Pete Reid, Cletus Rademacher, Ed A. Coon, Dr. Norman Brown, Tom W. Reed, J. W. Mendenhall, Lyle Wilson, Roger Barth, William T. Moore, Glenn Waugh, Dr. Robert Maris, Al Oldershaw, A. L. Sanderson, Len Peterson, Ernest Polwarth, Earl Morrison, George Yancey, Ed Hughes, Dr. George Anderson, Grover Wilson, Cameron Sherwood, George Ingraham, George C. Laue, Charles Gonser, Maage La Counte, De Witt Wallace, Sam Whittemore, William Freeman, Donald Sheehan, Donald Sherwood and Baker Ferguson. Harper was buried at Fairmount Memorial Park in a plot that Dorothy purchased adjoining that of the Brooks and the Mendenhalls.

Dorothy lived for 22 more years and remained active until her death on June 14, 1994. She had the support of her son Ed during those years, and also enjoyed visits from the other children when they were able to come to Spokane and Liberty Lake. She had another romantic interest for several years but told the author she was "glad that she hadn't married again." It would indeed have been hard to find someone to take Harper's place. Her grave lies next to Harper's at Fairmount.

**Harper Joy's headstone at Fairmount Memorial Park. Included are the words that were his personal credo: "Hold High the Torch."** *(Photo by Doris J. Woodward)*

# The Finale

As I write the finish to the Harper Joy story, I only have to look out my upstairs window to gaze down on the property that for so many years belonged to the Joy family, and I visualize the numerous children, from all over the South Hill, who reveled in the Cannon Hill & Pacific Railroad and to this day remember those good times.

I envision Ed Joy scrambling up the stone wall that still stands between the Joy property and mine, to visit his pal Bob Dillon (why use the sidewalk when there was a stone wall to climb?) The boys spent time at the Dillon house (now mine) watching television, because the Joys didn't have television for several years. If Harper had purchased a television set in those early days, he would have seen many of his colleagues from the world of vaudeville – and I wonder if Harper ever felt a pang of regret that he hadn't stayed in vaudeville and "made it big" like those performers.

I hope that he never regretted it, because his life and energy were concentrated, for so many years, on bringing pleasure to other people – to the people attending the circuses, to the war effort for which he raised unbelievable amounts of money, to the students who have filled the halls of Whitman College, and to the multitude of children who benefited and are still benefiting from the work of the Shriners. In the final analysis, although he certainly gave so much, he may have been the recipient of the greatest gift of all – that of being able to make people laugh.

He lived his life the way he chose and surely could not have regretted the happiness – or should I say joy – that he brought to others. With this, I salute Harper Joy.

## Encore

The new owners of the Joy house have remodeled the grand old place. During the process Ed Joy stopped by to talk to some men who were working outside. He asked them if they knew there used to be a railroad there in the backyard, and one of the men said, "Yeah, and I heard there were elephants too." Thus do legends get started! But come to think of it, I believe that if Harper could have figured out a way to do it, there would have been elephants too.

The above watercolor painting of Harper by Don Hattnor was found recently by Linda Joy, when she was looking through some old sheet music. She and Ed have no idea when or where it was painted. It seems almost serendipitous that it was found in time to be included in this book.

# SOURCES

Adoption Papers:

Adoption of Harry Hess. Petition No. 4461 filed June 16, 1884. Superior Court of the State of Washington.

Adoption of James Harper Lounsbury and Laura Irene Lounsbury. Petition No. 2796 filed January 4, 1898. Superior Court of the State of Washington.

Adoption of Laura Irene Lounsbury. Petition No. 2796 filed December 16, 1897 Superior Court of the State of Washington.

"Clowning Around at the Davenport Hotel." *Inland Northwest Homes & Lifetstyles*. October/November 2004.

*Crown Jewels*. Silent movie, Spokane, Washington: University Club, 1929. Available on DVD at the Archives, Northwest Museum of Arts & Culture, Spokane, Washington.

Douglas, William O. *The Early Years, Go East, Young Ma*n. New York City: Random House, 1900.

Edwards, G. Thomas. *The Triumph of Tradition, The Early Years of Whitman College 1859-1924*. Walla Walla: Whitman College, no date.

_____. *Traditions in a Turbulent Age, Whitman College 1925-1975*, Walla Walla: Whitman College, 2001.

Edwards, Jonathan. *An Illustrated History of Spokane County, State of Washington*. Spokane, WA: Eastern Washington Genealogical Society, 1900.

Fairmount Memorial Park, 5200 W. Wellesley Avenue, Spokane, Washington 992059797. Records of the Brook, Joy and Mendenhall families.

Harper Joy, guest on *This Is Your Life*. Tape of radio show aired on January 4, 1949. Ralph Edwards, Master of Ceremonies.

"Investment Executive Finds Enjoyment as a Circus Clown." Whitman Alumnus vol. 48, no. 5 (July 1964). Walla Walla: Whitman College Alumni Association.

Joy, James Richard, compiler. *Thomas Joy and his Descendants*. New York City, privately published, 1900.

Newspapers:

*Spokane Chronicle* (Spokane, Washington). Various issues on microfilm at the Spokane Public Library, Spokane, Washington.

*Spokesman-Review* (Spokane, Washington). Various issues, on microfilm at the Spokane Public Library, Spokane, Washington.

*Walla Walla Union Bulletin* (Walla Walla, Washington). Various issues, on microfilm at the Holland Library, Pullman, Washington.

Northwest Museum of Arts & Culture (MAC), 2316 W. First Avenue, Spokane, Washington 99201-1099.

Northwest Room, Spokane Public Library, 305 Main Street, Spokane, Washington.

Pierre Salinger biography. Online at <**nndb.com/people/011/000022942/**>. Program printed for the dedication of the Harper Joy Theatre. June 1967.

"Record of the College Years 1921-1922." The *Waiilatpu*, volume XI, March 1922.

*Spokane City Directories*, 1889-1930. Spokane, Wash: R. L. Polk Publishing Co., 1889-1930.

*The Scroll*, Alumni Magazine of Phi Delta Theta. Fall 1972. *Phi Delta Theta Fraternity*, 2 South Campus Ave., Oxford, Ohio 45056-1872.

Starr, Kimberly. "A Biography of Harper Joy." *HJT Encore*, vol. 2, no. 6. Theatre program for "The Marriage of Figaro."

The *Bankoscope*, Spokane and Eastern newsletter. February 1949, page 6.

Theologus, Ellen. "Nancy Joy: One Woman's Struggle To Find Her Own Way." *Columbia Flyer*, Vol. 7, No. 17, Oct. 2, 1975.

*The White Tops*. December-January 1932-1933. Publication of the Circus Fans of America.

Umatilla County Circuit Court, P.O. Box 1307, Pendleton, Oregon 97801.

United States Federal Censuses, 1850 through 1930. Databases online <**Ancestry.com**>.

United States Immigration Collection, New York Passenger Lists, 1920-1957. Database online at <Ancestry.com>.

Van der Loeff, A. Rutgers. Manuscript collection #MSSC 125. Archives, Northwest Museum of Arts & Culture, Spokane, Washington.

Walla Walla County Clerk, P.O. Box 836, Walla Walla, Washington 99362.

*Walla Walla County School Records*, 1883-1910. Walla Walla Valley Genealogical Society, 1998.

Walla Walla Valley Genealogical Society, P.O. Box 115, Walla Walla, Washington 99362-0003

Whitman College & Northwest Archives. Penrose Memorial Library, 345 Boyer Avenue, Walla Walla, Washington 99362.

Whitman College Speech and Debate Team. Online at <**www.whitman.edu/ rhetoric/history/1921.htm**>.

World War I Draft Registration Cards. 1917-1918. Online at <**Ancestry.com**>.

# INDEX